The
Apple of
His Eye

Published by Barbour Publishing, Inc., P.O. Box 719, Uhrichsville, Ohio 44683, www.barbourbooks.com

Our mission is to publish and distribute inspirational products offering exceptional value and biblical encouragement to the masses.

Member of the
Evangelical Christian
Publishers Association

Printed in China.

JoAnne Simmons

The Apple of His Eye

Becoming a Beautiful
Woman of God

BARBOUR
PUBLISHING

To Jodi and Lilly. . .
You are precious gifts, dreams come true.
I pray you become beautiful women of God.
I love you with every beat of my heart.

Contents

Introduction

Through salvation in Jesus Christ, every woman has the opportunity to be made perfect in God's sight, to be looked upon as beautiful by God, to be loved, cherished, and protected by Him. But neither clothes nor cosmetics, features nor figures make any difference to God, for "your beauty… should be that of your inner self, the unfading beauty of a gentle and quiet spirit, which is of great worth in God's sight" (1 Peter 3:3–4 NIV).

As you delve into the devotions of this book, may you find insight and encouragement in the light of God's Word for developing a lasting, inner beauty as the apple of His eye.

Jesus paid it all,
All to Him I owe;
Sin had left a crimson stain,
He washed it white as snow.

ELVINA M. HALL

A Beautiful Heart,
White as Snow

Stain Remover

"Come now, let us settle the matter,"
says the LORD. "Though your sins are like scarlet,
they shall be as white as snow; though they are
red as crimson, they shall be like wool."
ISAIAH 1:18 NIV

$\mathcal{A}$ splash of tomato sauce on a pretty white
sweater, or worse, a whole plate of spaghetti
dropped smack-dab in the middle of expensive
new carpet. . .stains are so frustrating and ugly.

The stain of sin is even uglier, and the very
first step to becoming a beautiful woman of
God is to remove it completely. But there's no
pre-wash spray or any amount of scrubbing
that will do. Good intentions, good words, good
deeds. . .they're nice but never enough. And what
is enough is so much simpler! Only God's grace
erases sin, through the death and resurrection of
Jesus, for "in him we have redemption through
his blood, the forgiveness of sins, in accordance

with the riches of God's grace that he lavished on us" (Ephesians 1:7–8 NIV).

It's kind of paradoxical that the bright red blood of Jesus is what washes scarlet sins away to make them white as snow, but it's really about the sacrifice Jesus made—His very life! In Old Testament times, God's people offered animals as a sacrifice, shedding their blood before God to atone for their sin. When Christ came and was crucified, His blood was shed once and for all to pay for sin and make righteous before God everyone who accepts and believes in the Savior.

If you have not done so already, let Jesus cleanse away your unsightly sin. Tell Him you believe in Him and His work on the cross to save you. Admit your sin and your need to be forgiven. Invite Him into your heart to make it truly beautiful and then live your life for Him, learning from and maturing in His Word. And then praise Him, for like the old hymn goes, "Jesus paid it all, all to Him I owe. Sin had left a crimson stain; He washed it white as snow."

No Blemish Too Big

Have mercy on me, O God, according to your steadfast love; according to your abundant mercy blot out my transgressions. Wash me thoroughly from my iniquity, and cleanse me from my sin! Purge me with hyssop, and I shall be clean; wash me, and I shall be whiter than snow.

PSALM 51:1–2, 7 ESV

Too many women might believe that God's grace is just for "little" sins, that only good girls can become Christians, that they have too dark and wild a past and/or present to ever be forgiven. But the Bible says, "Do not be deceived: neither the sexually immoral, nor idolaters, nor adulterers, nor men who practice homosexuality, nor thieves, nor the greedy, nor drunkards, nor revilers, nor swindlers will inherit the kingdom of God. And such were some of you. But you were washed, you were sanctified, you were justified in the name of the Lord Jesus Christ and by the Spirit of our God" (1 Corinthians 6:9-11 ESV). The key there is that the apostle Paul is addressing people who had committed all these sins—"And such were some of you"—but were washed clean, completely forgiven of them and would, in fact, inherit the kingdom of God. Paul's life, too, is an incredible testimony to the grace of God, a perfect example that no blemish is too big for God to forgive, for Paul had been a persecutor and murderer of Christians.

Other women have anger issues with God— they blame Him for the blemishes inflicted on them by others. It's certainly hard to understand why God doesn't intervene in all cases of abuse, neglect, and mistreatment. But we must remember that our world is fallen, but God is good; and His ways are not our ways, but He can bring good out of anything.

Without a doubt, there is no blemish too big for God to forgive and to use for His glory. And a beautiful heart is one that has asked God's forgiveness of these blemishes and seeks His help in forgiving others, too.

Spa Treatment

Therefore, if anyone is in Christ, he is a new creation.
The old has passed away; behold, the new has come.
2 CORINTHIANS 5:17 ESV

A new hairstyle, a manicure and pedicure, an hour-long massage—these are all fantastic ways to feel beautiful and rejuvenated. But they're only temporary fixes for human features that are aging and wasting away.

Lasting revitalization comes from accepting Jesus as Savior; it's like getting full-spa treatment for the heart and soul. It's freedom from regret and guilt. It's letting go of the past, no matter how dark it might have been. It's realizing a new purpose for life. It's discovering real hope for eternity in heaven. It's feeling peace where anxiety once ruled. It's being refreshed, encouraged, and guided by the Holy Spirit. It's becoming beautiful from the inside out.

Better yet, these heart-and-soul spa treatments for followers of Christ don't cost a cent; they are free and unlimited, paid for by God's grace. And while they don't cause perfection or an end to all stress, they do include daily renewal (Lamentations 3:22–23), strength training (Philippians 4:13), a personal relationship with the greatest King of all time (Revelation 19) and a reservation for forever with Him in paradise (John 14:1–3), where everyone will have picture-perfect, ageless bodies (1 Corinthians 15:35–44).

And because of the heart-and-soul spa found in Jesus Christ, "we do not lose heart. Though outwardly we are wasting away, yet inwardly we are being renewed day by day. For our light and momentary troubles are achieving for us an eternal glory that far outweighs them all. So we fix our eyes not on what is seen, but on what is unseen, since what is seen is temporary, but what is unseen is eternal" (2 Corinthians 4:16–18 NIV).

Spin Cycle

I want to do what is good, but I don't.
I don't want to do what is wrong, but I do it anyway.
ROMANS 7:19 NLT

Until heaven, where everyone will be perfect, unfortunately Christians still get stuck on spin cycles of sin. Forgiven, yes, but still struggling with a human nature that makes mistakes and requires repentance *every single* day. It's easy to get discouraged by this and wonder how on earth God doesn't get completely fed up!

Even the apostle Paul struggled with this and said, "I don't really understand myself, for I want to do what is right, but I don't do it. Instead, I do what I hate. . . . And I know that nothing good lives in me, that is, in my sinful nature. I want to do what is right, but I can't. I want to do what is good, but I don't. I don't want to do what is wrong, but I do it anyway. But if I do what I don't want to do, I am not really the one doing wrong; it is sin living in me that does it. I have discovered this principle of life—that when I want to do what is right, I inevitably do what is wrong. I love God's law with all my heart. But there is another power within me that is at war with my mind. This power makes me a slave to the sin that is still within me. Oh, what a miserable person I am! Who will free me from this life that is dominated by sin and death? Thank God! The answer is in Jesus Christ our Lord" (Romans 7:15, 18–25 NLT).

A beautiful heart is not a perfect heart; it's a *forgiven* heart—a heart that knows Jesus is the only hope of salvation, a heart that knows that the round-and-round spin cycle of sin here on earth will one day finally halt forever in our heavenly home.

Wearing White

Wash your hands, you sinners; purify your hearts,
for your loyalty is divided between God and the world.
JAMES 4:8 NLT

There are obvious places where wearing white is not a wise fashion choice, like on dusty bleachers cheering for a baseball game. There are obvious activities to avoid while wearing white, such as pulling weeds in a flower bed. There are also obvious people to avoid while wearing white, say, for example, a toddler with a sticky fist full of strawberries.

Likewise, beautiful women of God must be careful to avoid certain people, places, and situations that tempt them to sin, in order to keep clean. Not because God will ever stop forgiving—He won't—but because of the self-inflicted harm that results from rolling around in the dirt of sin. Playing with sinful situations, people, and places is like playing with fire. It's nearly impossible to not get burned. The enemy, Satan, is out for blood, and he will use every method he can to devour Christians, hoping to cause us to fall away from our Savior and suffer.

It's not about shutting ourselves off like hermits; it's about being in the world but not of the world (Romans 12:2). It's not about avoiding hurting, sinful people; but it's about helping them up, not letting them pull us down (2 Corinthians 6:14–16). It's about drawing close to the Lord for protection and peace as we live our lives in a fallen world. And it's about *fleeing* from the opportunities that we know will lead us into temptation and sin.

A beautiful woman of God is wearing white. God washes her sin away and makes her like snow, and it's His desire that she stay pure (1 Peter 1:14–16). Contrary to popular belief, it's not because He's a killjoy. It's because only He can see beyond the deceiving facade of sin to the filth that's festering just behind it, a filth that is strong and sticky and all too easy to get bogged down in.

Beautiful Tears

Let there be tears for what you have done. Let there be sorrow and deep grief. Let there be sadness instead of laughter, and gloom instead of joy. Humble yourselves before the Lord, and he will lift you up in honor.
JAMES 4:9–10 NLT

Red eyes and running mascara aren't typically considered attractive. But when they result from tears cried in repentance of sin, they truly are beautiful in God's sight. In 2 Corinthians 7:8–10, the apostle Paul explains to the believers of Corinth a little more about this type of sorrow: "I am not sorry that I sent that severe letter to you, though I was sorry at first, for I know it was painful to you for a little while. Now I am glad I sent it, not because it hurt you, but because the pain caused you to repent and change your ways. It was the kind of sorrow God wants his people to have, so you were not harmed by us in any way. For the kind of sorrow God wants us to experience leads us away from sin and results in salvation" (NLT).

God does not delight in the pain of His people, but He *does* want them to hurt over sin. Sin draws us away from God. If we realize the pain of it and repent of it, we come back into fellowship with Him. And remembering the pain of sin helps us avoid it in the future, helps us draw closer to God so He can protect us from it.

Like James talks about in 4:9–10, we should have tears for the wrong we have done, and those tears are beautiful because when we humble ourselves and repent of our sins, God will lift us up in honor.

Rinse and Repeat

If we confess our sins, he is faithful and just to forgive us our sins and to cleanse us from all unrighteousness.
1 John 1:9 esv

Sort of like the instructions to "rinse and repeat" on a bottle of shampoo, we need to ask God to rinse our sins away and repeat again and again and again, because we're constantly guilty of sin. Thankfully God's cleansing shampoo never runs out; He forgives us every time we ask. And difficult as it might be, He wants us to forgive others in the same way. In Matthew 18:21–22 (esv), Peter asked Jesus about forgiving others: " 'Lord, how often will my brother sin against me, and I forgive him? As many as seven times?' Jesus said to him, 'I do not say to you seven times, but seventy-seven times.' "

And again in Luke 17:3–4 (esv), "If your brother sins, rebuke him, and if he repents, forgive him, and if he sins against you seven times in the day, and turns to you seven times, saying, 'I repent,' you must forgive him."

It's so hard to let go of the hurt when others do us wrong. We want the offender to suffer, too. But every time someone asks for forgiveness, we need to remember all the wrongs of ours that God has forgotten. We need to think about what a beautiful relief it is to know we're truly forgiven. Our gratitude for that should be so great that we just can't help but want to extend forgiveness to others, too. And our willingness to forgive should reflect that of our gracious heavenly Father.

Relying on and imitating God's ability to "rinse and repeat" will truly make us beautiful.

Bruises Aren't Beautiful

You, dear children, are from God and have overcome them,
because the one who is in you is greater
than the one who is in the world.

1 JOHN 4:4 NIV

Scripture is clear that we have an enemy, the devil, who hates us and wants to destroy us (Ephesians 6:11–18; 1 Peter 5:8–9). He never wants anyone to know the forgiveness and salvation found in Jesus Christ (2 Corinthians 4:4). And for those who do, he still tries to tear us down and beat us up; he wants to tempt us to sin and keep us there and thus out of fellowship with God. He is often successful through the lies he tells us, the lies we too easily believe, the lies we beat ourselves up with.

The Bible says of the devil, "There is no truth in him. When he lies, he speaks out of his own character, for he is a liar and the father of lies" (John 8:44 ESV). The devil wants us to think that God won't forgive us. He whispers horribly false things into our minds when we know we've messed up yet again, things like "God is fed up with you by now! Don't even bother praying. There is nothing good in you, so you might as well just keep on being bad." It's a daily battle, but we have to resist these lies.

Bruises aren't beautiful. God does not want us to beat ourselves up over our sins; He wants to remove them from us. Psalm 103:12 (KJV) says, "As far as the east is from the west, so far hath he removed our transgressions from us."

A beautiful woman of God can repent, confident that God forgives, and then learn from her mistakes and move on, maturing in her faith and trusting that she can overcome the devil's lies, because the beautiful, powerful truth is that He who is in us is greater than the one who is in the world.

Refresh

Now repent of your sins and turn to God, so that your sins may be wiped away. Then times of refreshment will come from the presence of the Lord.

Acts 3:19–20 NLT

Just a little white lie here, a tiny bit of gossip over there. Maybe a bit of a bad attitude and, okay, a whole lot of impatience. Sometimes, especially with "little" sins, we think repenting isn't really necessary. Maybe a lot of the little things we do don't seem so bad, but if we stop to really think about them, we know they're sins. We don't want to admit when we're messing up; we don't want to be vulnerable before God and ask Him to help change a bad attitude or habit or behavior.

But over time, unconfessed sin becomes ugly and its burden so heavy. Why do we ever think we should hang on to it?

So much better than taking the most relaxing bubble bath, repenting and turning our sins over to God so that they can be wiped away will bring times of refreshment in the presence of the Lord (Acts 3:19–20). This scripture may literally be referring to when Jesus comes back again, and His people will certainly be refreshed for eternity in His presence! Until then, we need to let God refresh us daily by repenting of all our sins. We need to give our Savior all our sins and burdens, for He said, "Come to me, all who labor and are heavy laden, and I will give you rest. Take my yoke upon you, and learn from me, for I am gentle and lowly in heart, and you will find rest for your souls. For my yoke is easy, and my burden is light" (Matthew 11:28–30 ESV).

Easy and light! What a beautifully refreshing promise!

Soul Sisters

Two are better than one, because they
have a good return for their labor:
If either of them falls down, one can help the other up.
ECCLESIASTES 4:9–10 NIV

A true friend would never fail to tell you about the speck of spinach stuck in your teeth or a mortifying piece of toilet paper trailing off your high heel. She doesn't mind one bit if your house is a wreck, and she's welcome to pop in at any time. She's seen you at your worst and best and has shown you she's loyal through thick and thin. She'll be honest if your haircut is hideous and give you a real answer to "Does this make me look fat?"

More importantly, though, as a Christian, a true friend is someone who will keep you grooming your inner beauty that comes from being a daughter of the King of kings.

If you don't already have one, pray that God will lead you to a female friend who will keep you accountable in your faith. Someone you can pray with and confide in. Someone who will challenge and encourage you, and in turn you can do the same for her. Someone you can simply have fun with, too! Charles Swindoll once said, "I cannot even imagine where I would be today were it not for that handful of friends who have given me a heart full of joy. Let's face it, friends make life a lot more fun."

Every beautiful woman of God needs another beautiful woman in her life. A faithful friend, a fellow believer, another woman who has become a child of God through Jesus Christ. We all need a soul sister who will help us keep our hearts free from sin and white as snow.

Without Christ there is no hope.

CHARLES SPURGEON

Beautiful Eyes,
Full of Hope

Makeup and Color

Praise be to the God and Father of our Lord Jesus Christ!
In his great mercy he has given us new birth
into a living hope through the resurrection
of Jesus Christ from the dead.

1 PETER 1:3 NIV

The most beautiful eyes are not the ones perfectly outlined with liner and mascara, highlighted with sparkly shadow. Nor are they the ones with the most gorgeous, vivid colors, whether blue, green, brown, hazel, or a pretty combination. Their beauty fades instantly if they are clouded with doubt and worry, discouragement and hopelessness. What causes those clouds in so many eyes? It's the sin of this fallen world, sin that we so desperately need to be saved from.

Eyes that are truly beautiful are the ones that are clear and bright because they have seen the need for a Savior and have accepted Jesus Christ. These eyes are full of real hope, the unwavering hope that comes from knowing Christ conquered sin and death (1 Corinthians 15:57), has overcome the world (John 16:33), and is preparing an eternal paradise for all who believe in Him (John 14:1–3).

Eyes that are truly beautiful are the ones turned upon Jesus. They filter everything they see through the light of His love and His promises, and they reflect Him, shining clarity and hope into the dark world around them. They choose to focus on Jesus above all, no matter what pleasant or painful circumstances might be going on around them.

The very best beauty tip for gorgeous eyes is found in an old hymn that goes, "Turn your eyes upon Jesus. Look full in His wonderful face, and the things of earth will grow strangely dim in the light of His glory and grace."

Confident

Rejoice in our confident hope.
ROMANS 12:12 NLT

The eyes of a woman of God are confident eyes, confident because the hope they have is proven and true because their *source* of hope, Jesus Christ, is proven and true. He is the Savior whom God promised to all people, sent to live among us and minister to us and then die and rise again, taking our sin upon Himself and providing our justification before God. "God made him who had no sin to be sin for us, so that in him we might become the righteousness of God" (2 Corinthians 5:21 NIV).

No other religion can provide the hope of a Savior like Jesus. No other purpose or pursuit can provide the assurance of eternal life with God in heaven. Jesus said, "I am the way, the truth, and the life. No one comes to the Father except through Me" (John 14:6 NKJV). Critics might want to mock those words as simply that, just words, fictional words that come from an ancient piece of literature. But throughout history Christ has been proven again and again in the biblical prophecies He fulfilled, in the evidence of His death, and in the countless lives He has transformed and is transforming when people choose to put their faith in Him.

Even the most confident eyes occasionally flash a doubt or two during difficult times, but always, *always* the eyes that sincerely look to Jesus as their source of hope will be able to refocus their attention on the confidence they have in Christ.

Always Looking Up

---

*I lift up my eyes to the mountains—where does my
help come from? My help comes from the LORD,
the Maker of heaven and earth.*
PSALM 121:1–2 NIV

Beautiful eyes are always looking up, both
literally and figuratively. A beautiful woman of
God has great confidence in her heavenly Father,
the almighty Creator of all things. When the pain
and problems of life become overwhelming, she
might be looking low for a little while. But she
remembers to ask herself, "Why are you cast
down, O my soul, and why are you in turmoil
within me? Hope in God; for I shall again praise
him, my salvation and my God" (Psalm 43:5 ESV).
She must choose to have faith that heavenly help
is on its way because God promises in His Word
that it is.

Beautiful women of God have eyes that

look up toward heaven with optimism. They attract and encourage others with their positive perspective. While many are seeing everything in a negative light, the eyes of a godly woman are trying to see the best in things; they're always looking for the silver lining, and even in the worst of circumstances they are choosing to focus on the good and the glory to God that might result and the blessings in the midst of storms.

Catherine Marshall once said, "God is the only one who can make the valley of trouble a door of hope." Beautiful women have eyes that look up out of every valley with expectancy, knowing that God is able to do so much more than we can ask or imagine (Ephesians 3:20), and that He will help us and provide for us in His wise and perfect timing.

A Heavenly Home

But we are citizens of heaven,
where the Lord Jesus Christ lives.
And we are eagerly waiting for him
to return as our Savior.

PHILIPPIANS 3:20 NLT

❧

This world is not our home—that's something a woman who is lovely in the eyes of God can be glad about. While there's still much good in God's creation and in His people, ultimately sin is making quite an ugly mess here. And at any given moment her own personal home might be in a state of destruction and deterioration, too—especially if she shares it with small children! A beautiful woman of God can delight and take hope in the fact that because of Jesus, her real and permanent (and clean!) home is in heaven.

Beautiful eyes are those that look around this world and know it's only temporary. They see things in light of the welcoming, warm glow that shines from the door of a heavenly home, a place Jesus has been preparing. He encourages His people in John 14:1–2 (NLT), "Don't let your hearts be troubled. Trust in God, and trust also in me. There is more than enough room in my Father's home. If this were not so, would I have told you that I am going to prepare a place for you?"

Stop to imagine for a moment what kind of place the King of kings must be preparing for His children! What splendor there must be! If we choose to focus on the glory of heaven, then as we look around at what might be less-than-stellar surroundings, we can find the will to wait patiently. One day this world will be replaced with God's perfect new kingdom, and our time here is just a blink of one beautiful eye compared to timeless eternity.

On Alert

"However, no one knows the day or hour when these things will happen, not even the angels in heaven or the Son himself. Only the Father knows. And since you don't know when that time will come, be on guard! Stay alert!"

MARK 13:32–33 NLT

Mothers are sometimes described as having eyes in the backs of their heads. Miraculously at times, it seems they somehow know exactly when one of their children is up to something. They are always on the alert when it comes to their kiddos.

A beautiful woman of God is also on alert for her Savior. She knows Jesus came once and He is coming back again. Her hopeful eyes are always watching for the signs of His glorious return, for Jesus said, "And there will be signs in sun and moon and stars, and on the earth distress of nations in perplexity because of the roaring of the sea and the waves, people fainting with fear and with foreboding of what is coming on the world. For the powers of the heavens will be shaken. And then they will see the Son of Man coming in a cloud with power and great glory. Now when these things begin to take place, straighten up and raise your heads, because your redemption is drawing near" (Luke 21:25–28 ESV).

For some, scriptures like these cause fear and anxiety. They wonder how this will all play out, what persecution and danger they might experience in the end times. No one has all the answers to the many questions this topic raises, but Christians should stand up and lift their heads, for their redemption is drawing near. There is no need for a beautiful woman of God to cower with her eyes down, hoping no one notices her. No, she should stand up tall and be on alert with excitement and expectation, for Jesus *is* coming back, and He is her hope and salvation.

A Look Inside

"The LORD looks at the heart."
1 SAMUEL 16:7 NKJV

⁓

The world today is so focused on the outer image. It can be so discouraging to look at all the magazine covers in the checkout line at the grocery store and wonder how on earth to ever measure up to the gorgeous, glamorous models featured there. But God's ways are not the world's ways (Isaiah 55:8), and scripture says, "Man looks at the outward appearance, but the LORD looks at the heart" (1 Samuel 16:7 NKJV).

The fact is, we are all aging and our bodies are deteriorating. We can't possibly fully maintain the health and beauty of youth, no matter how hard we try.

For this and many other reasons, a beautiful woman of God trains her eyes to look for the inner beauty in people, not only when looking for a spouse but also in developing loving relationships with and caring for those around her.

It's not always easy to look for the inner beauty in people who might, for example, not have clean clothes or good hygiene, but God says He looks at the heart, and we should, too. Consider what James says about those who might not look nice on the outside: "How can you claim to have faith in our glorious Lord Jesus Christ if you favor some people over others? For example, suppose someone comes into your meeting dressed in fancy clothes and expensive jewelry, and another comes in who is poor and dressed in dirty clothes. If you give special attention and a good seat to the rich person, but you say to the poor one, 'You can stand over there, or else sit on the floor'—well, doesn't this discrimination show that your judgments are guided by evil motives? Listen to me, dear brothers and sisters. Hasn't God chosen the poor in this world to be rich in faith? Aren't they the ones who will inherit the Kingdom he promised to those who love him?" (James 2:1–5 NLT).

Because He offers hope to everyone no matter their outward appearance, God looks at the hearts of people, and so should the eyes of His beautiful daughters.

Avid Reader

You are my hiding place and my shield;
I hope in your word.
Psalm 119:114 ESV

There is an overload of information today, everywhere we look. On cell phones, tablets, and computers; through social media and texting; and on TVs in homes, restaurants, and stores, just to name a few! With all that is thrown at our eyes constantly in this world (much of which directly opposes what the Bible teaches), if we want to be beautiful to God, we need to make sure we are spending daily time with our eyes focused on God's Word, learning from and being lifted up by His truth.

God's Word is what directs our paths and shows us the way. The psalmist says, "Thy word is a lamp unto my feet, and a light unto my path. I have sworn, and I will perform it, that I will keep thy righteous judgments" (Psalm 119:105–106 KJV). And it's not enough to simply read it; we must meditate on it, memorize it, and apply it to our lives. Not because it's just a nice piece of literature to have knowledge of, but because "the word of God is quick, and powerful, and sharper than any twoedged sword, piercing even to the dividing asunder of soul and spirit, and of the joints and marrow, and is a discerner of the thoughts and intents of the heart" (Hebrews 4:12 KJV). God's Word is also part of the armor of God, which is what protects us and helps us fight against evil in this sinful world. Ephesians 6:17 (NLT) urges us to "take the sword of the Spirit, which is the word of God."

A beautiful woman of God has eyes full of hope because she focuses them regularly on the truth of God's Word.

Closed in Prayer

Rejoice evermore. Pray without ceasing.
In every thing give thanks: for this is the will
of God in Christ Jesus concerning you.
1 Thessalonians 5:16–18 kjv

---

*O*ften the eyes of a beautiful woman of God are not even open because they are closed in prayer—literally and sometimes in a more figurative sense because we all know there are many times when it's not possible to actually close our eyes in prayer. (Any woman who has had a near miss in heavy traffic or has a toddler who likes to climb will attest to that!)

Unfortunately the very real power of prayer is too often forgotten. If we would stop to focus on just who it is we're praying to—the almighty, all-powerful Creator God!—maybe we would spend less time worrying about our problems and more time bringing them to Him and *giving* them to Him (1 Peter 5:7). Why do we ever try to handle them on our own when we have such a great and powerful God, who through Jesus says, "Come to me, all you who are weary and burdened, and I will give you rest. Take my yoke upon you and learn from me, for I am gentle and humble in heart, and you will find rest for your souls. For my yoke is easy and my burden is light" (Matthew 11:28–30 NIV)?

When a woman of God begins to show signs of anxiety in her eyes, she knows to simply close them in prayer, turn her worries over to God, and hope in the promises of His Word, especially "Do not be anxious about anything, but in every situation, by prayer and petition, with thanksgiving, present your requests to God. And the peace of God, which transcends all understanding, will guard your hearts and your minds in Christ Jesus" (Philippians 4:6–7 NIV).

Window Shopping

So we fix our eyes not on what is seen,
but on what is unseen, since what is seen is temporary,
but what is unseen is eternal.
2 CORINTHIANS 4:18 NIV

It's way too tempting to visit the mall sometimes, no matter how good our intention to just "window shop" might be. There are so many nice things to buy (sales on them, even!), but a godly woman constantly needs to ask herself, "Do I really need this?" She uses her eyes to look for *needs* more than *wants*, especially when it comes to the things of this world. She knows that everything material here is just temporary, and so a better goal than accumulating worldly wealth and items is to store up treasure in heaven that will last for eternity. Matthew 6:19–21 (ESV) says, "Do not lay up for yourselves treasures on earth, where moth and rust destroy and where thieves break in and steal, but lay up for yourselves treasures in heaven, where neither moth nor rust destroys and where thieves do not break in and steal. For where your treasure is, there your heart will be also."

A beautiful woman of God also sees the needs of others as more important than her own. That's so much easier said than done and goes against our selfish human nature. But God's Word says, "Do nothing out of selfish ambition or vain conceit. Rather, in humility value others above yourselves, not looking to your own interests but each of you to the interests of the others" (Philippians 2:3–4 NIV).

It's not that God doesn't want us to enjoy the beauty and the things around us, but He wants us to be good stewards (Matthew 25:21–22), knowing that things here won't last and what's in heaven will last forever. It's wisest to do mostly window shopping in this life—just looking and not buying into the materialism of our world— because in our heavenly home, the eternal treasures will be so much better.

In our manner of speech, our plans of living, our dealings with others, our conduct and walk in the church and out of it—all should be done as becomes the Gospel.

ALBERT BARNES

Beautiful Lips,
Speaking in Love

Dramatic Impact

Let the words of my mouth, and the meditation of my heart, be acceptable in thy sight, O LORD, my strength, and my redeemer.
PSALM 19:14 KJV

We've all heard the saying, "Sticks and stones may break my bones, but words can never hurt me." It's a nice attempt at self-defense on a school playground, but it's just not true! Words absolutely hurt, and their effects are sometimes so much more damaging and long lasting than a physical wound. A woman of God keeps her lips truly beautiful by remembering the dramatic impact words can have and constantly striving to speak in love.

James describes the power of the tongue like this: "For if we could control our tongues, we would be perfect and could also control ourselves in every other way. We can make a large horse go wherever we want by means of a small bit in its mouth. And a small rudder makes a huge ship turn wherever the pilot chooses to go, even though the winds are strong. In the same way, the tongue is a small thing that makes grand speeches. But a tiny spark can set a great forest on fire. And the tongue is a flame of fire. It is a whole world of wickedness, corrupting your entire body. It can set your whole life on fire, for it is set on fire by hell itself" (James 3:2–6 NLT).

Wow! That's a heavy scripture passage and one we should think about every time we speak. "If we could control our tongues, we would be perfect." No, it's not possible in our sinful human nature to be completely perfect—that's why we need Jesus to make us perfect (2 Corinthians 5:18–21)—but as Christians we are held to a higher standard (1 Peter 1:16), and we should constantly be at least trying to control what we say. Only then will we have truly beautiful lips, because no amount of gloss or liner, color or moisturizer can improve the looks of a mouth that continually speaks ugly or hateful things.

Lying Lips

The LORD *detests lying lips,*
but he delights in people who are trustworthy.
PROVERBS 12:22 NIV

Little white lies, and big lies, too, are about
as common as the air we breathe these days.
Sadly, so many people just don't see the value of
telling the truth anymore. (Consider the state of
American politics today as just one unfortunate
example.) Not so with a beautiful woman of God.
If she wants to keep her lips beautiful, she will
speak the truth and only the truth, so help her
God—for we really do need His help!

A woman becomes truly beautiful when
she asks Jesus to be her Savior, becomes a new
creation, and begins to put to death the things
of her sinful nature, including lying and ugly
language from her lips. Consider Colossians
3:1–10 (NIV): "Since, then, you have been raised

with Christ, set your hearts on things above, where Christ is, seated at the right hand of God. Set your minds on things above, not on earthly things. For you died, and your life is now hidden with Christ in God. When Christ, who is your life, appears, then you also will appear with him in glory. Put to death, therefore, whatever belongs to your earthly nature: sexual immorality, impurity, lust, evil desires and greed, which is idolatry. Because of these, the wrath of God is coming. You used to walk in these ways, in the life you once lived. But now you must also rid yourselves of all such things as these: anger, rage, malice, slander, and filthy language from your lips. Do not lie to each other, since you have taken off your old self with its practices and have put on the new self, which is being renewed in knowledge in the image of its Creator."

Lying lips are never pretty, and a woman of God will do her best to rid herself of them. She will value the truth and speak it always.

Gossip Hurts

---

*Whoever keeps his mouth and his tongue
keeps himself out of trouble.*
PROVERBS 21:23 ESV

---

*E*rma Bombeck once said, "Some say our
national pastime is baseball. Not me. It's gossip."
Isn't that the painful truth? No matter how we
like to disguise it—maybe as just "chatting"
about someone, or "venting frustration" about a
coworker, or even "sharing" a (much-too-detailed)
prayer request—we are all guilty of gossip at one
time or another, maybe even daily. And it's such
a hard habit to break. But a beautiful woman of
God needs to make it a priority to guard her lips
when it comes to participating in and spreading
gossip. Why? Well, consider this question that
the psalmist poses: "Who may worship in your
sanctuary, LORD? Who may enter your presence
on your holy hill?" The answer? "Those who lead

blameless lives and do what is right, speaking the truth from sincere hearts. Those who refuse to gossip or harm their neighbors or speak evil of their friends" (Psalm 15:1–3 NLT).

The hard bottom line is, our gossip about others negatively affects our relationship with God. We may think it's just harmless chatter until we consider that passage from Psalms, and of course until we are the subject of the gossip.

A little tip to help break the stubborn habit of gossip, to guard what you say about others and make sure that everything said is something you would say in their presence, is this: Before you begin talking about another person, stop to imagine that the conversation will be recorded— because, honestly, in this age of smartphones (many of which include video cameras), it very well could be. Make sure that every conversation you have is one that could be recorded and played back without remorse.

Gossip hurts others and leaves ugly stains on the lips, the mouth, the heart. Worse, it distances us from our heavenly Father. A woman who desires spiritual beauty does her very best to avoid it!

Encouraging

Encourage one another daily.
HEBREWS 3:13 NIV

*J*ust like the power of words to hurt is extreme, the power of them to help and encourage is tremendous, too. Sometimes all it takes is an encouraging word or note or phone call or text or e-mail to keep someone going during a rough time.

What are some practical ways for a woman who is lovely before God to encourage others with her words? Offer empathy and helpful counsel if you have been through a similar situation; point out the positives in the circumstances from a more objective perspective; compliment a friend or loved one on what he or she is doing well; share other good things you've heard said about the person; and, yes, even just compliment a friend's appearance to help make her day! Most importantly, share encouraging scriptures with others, especially ones that remind that someday we'll be in heaven with God for eternity, like 1 Thessalonians 4:17–18 (NIV): "And so we will be with the Lord forever. Therefore encourage one another with these words."

Paul instructs in 1 Thessalonians 5:11 (NIV), "Encourage one another and build each other up," and Hebrews 3:13 tell us to encourage *daily*. That's something we forget about too easily, to encourage one another *every single day*. It's such a simple thing to offer kind words, yet too often we only do so when we're aware someone is going through a rough time. As beautiful women of God (many of whom have the gift of gab!) we need to proactively use our words to speak encouragement into the lives of those around us. It will build us up as much as it does them, and it's another important way to make our lips truly beautiful.

Full of Praise

Praise the LORD!
PSALM 150:1 ESV

❧

A woman of God makes her lips so much more beautiful if she chooses to honor God with her words, especially in praise to Him. Psalm 150 (ESV) is an excellent reminder and a great scripture passage to memorize and offer up to God with a sincere heart every day:

> Praise the LORD!
> Praise God in his sanctuary;
> praise him in his mighty heavens!
> Praise him for his mighty deeds;
> praise him according to his excellent
>   greatness!
> Praise him with trumpet sound;
> praise him with lute and harp!
> Praise him with tambourine and dance;

praise him with strings and pipe!
Praise him with sounding cymbals;
praise him with loud clashing cymbals!
Let everything that has breath praise the
    Lord!
Praise the Lord!

If we make this our prayer each morning
as we start our day, imagine the improved
perspective we could have no matter what our
circumstances might be, no matter the state of
our home, or the hungry children to feed, or the
pile of work waiting for us. Let's choose to begin
the day with, "I praise You, Lord! I praise You in
Your sanctuary, in Your mighty heavens. I praise
You for Your mighty deeds and Your excellent
greatness. I will praise You with all that I am and
with everything I have!" Whether singing that or
speaking it or even simply whispering it in our
souls, we will be uplifted and encouraged by the
fact that we have an almighty God who loves and
cares for us and who is worthy of all praise. Our
lips can choose nothing better to say than words
and songs that praise the Lord.

Give Thanks

In every thing give thanks.
1 THESSALONIANS 5:18 KJV

In the aftermath of the horrific September 11 attacks on the World Trade Center, there were some fascinating stories of people who, had their mornings gone as planned, should have been at work in the towers when they went down— but they were not because of some seeming inconvenience like being stuck in traffic or some other delay. Imagine the perspective those people now have when something unexpected hinders their intended plans. They probably give thanks for such interruptions.

A woman of God should constantly be speaking thanks, no matter what her circumstances, because she can't possibly see all the details of how God might be using them to protect her; to provide for her; to strengthen, discipline, and mature her; and to ultimately accomplish His will. According to 1 Thessalonians 5:18 (ESV), we are to "give thanks in all circumstances," not just those that we like and that are part of our plans.

We can adopt a negative attitude, complaining when every tiny detail doesn't go our way, or we can embrace an attitude of gratitude, choosing to focus on the blessings we've been given and literally counting them aloud to gain a good perspective. And we can take time to thank others in our lives for even the smallest of gestures, because a little thankfulness and kindness go a long way in encouraging others and shining the light of God's love.

To have truly beautiful lips, a woman of God will use them rarely to grumble and much more frequently to express her gratitude.

All Kinds of Prayer

---

*And pray in the Spirit on all occasions with
all kinds of prayers and requests.
With this in mind, be alert and always
keep on praying for all the Lord's people.*
EPHESIANS 6:18 NIV

The very best thing we can do with our lips is
to use them in prayer. The Bible tells us to do
so on all occasions with all kinds of prayers and
requests. There is nothing we can't bring before
God to ask for His help. Philippians 4:6 (NLT)
tells us not to "worry about anything; instead,
pray about everything. Tell God what you need,
and thank him for all he has done."

Jesus Himself instructs us how to pray in the
Bible. Matthew 6 teaches us a lot about prayer,
especially with the Lord's Prayer that we should
model:

Our Father in heaven,
may your name be kept holy.
May your Kingdom come soon.
May your will be done on earth,
as it is in heaven.
Give us today the food we need,
and forgive us our sins,
as we have forgiven those who sin against us.
And don't let us yield to temptation,
but rescue us from the evil one. (verses 9–13 NLT)

Our prayers should include praise and reverence for God, prayer for His will, requests for what we need, forgiveness of sins for ourselves, and help in forgiving others and avoiding sin.

A woman who has a thriving prayer life with praise and requests constantly on her lips in a continuing conversation with her heavenly Father is beautiful to the Lord. She knows He is her source of strength and hope and that all she needs to do is ask for His help and wisdom and He will give it for every circumstance of life.

Wholesome Talk

---

*Do not let any unwholesome talk come out of your mouths,
but only what is helpful for building others up according
to their needs, that it may benefit those who listen.*

EPHESIANS 4:29 NIV

Hearing four-letter words and ugly, crass
language seems completely unavoidable these days.
But as Paul says in Ephesians 4:29, we should not
participate in "unwholesome" talk, or as another
translation of the verse puts it, "Don't use foul
or abusive language. Let everything you say be
good and helpful, so that your words will be an
encouragement to those who hear them" (NLT).

It's a tough command to follow. What goes
in is what comes out, and when we hear so much
unwholesome talk around us every day, it's hard
to not repeat it—especially when we're upset.
Our first step is to try to control how much we
hear it. We can't control what others say, but we

can control how much we hear it on TV, on the radio, and in music and movies. We can choose not to bring movies into our homes that contain excessive bad language. We can change the station when we hear nasty language on the radio.

Using foul words may not seem like a big deal, but they are just that—foul, *ugly*—and a woman of God should strive to keep her lips beautiful, not mar them with unpleasant words. The truth is, our words say a lot about who we are as a person. Jesus Himself said, "Out of the abundance of the heart the mouth speaks" (Matthew 12:34 ESV). If we want our words to reflect a heart made beautiful by God's love, if we want pretty lips, then we will watch what we say and avoid unwholesome talk.

Guarded Lips

Set a watch, O Lord, before my mouth;
keep the door of my lips.
Psalm 141:3 kjv

❧

If we don't have it ourselves, then we all know women who have the gift of gab. For the most part, we women love to talk. Even the quieter ones among us likely have a few close friends or family members to chat a mile a minute with. Those who *are* on the quiet side actually have the advantage when it comes to one aspect of being a beautiful woman of God—being slow to speak. James instructs us in the Bible, "My dear brothers and sisters, take note of this: Everyone should be quick to listen, slow to speak and slow to become angry" (James 1:19 niv).

When we're talking too fast, it's far too easy to say things we might regret, like insulting or judgmental comments, a bit of gossip, or a little white lie. If we slow down a bit, take time to listen to others, and really think before we respond, or simply think wisely before we start a conversation, then we do much better to keep our lips and words beautiful and pleasing to God.

Controlling your tongue is certainly one of the hardest disciplines of all, but as you pray and seek to do better, here are several proverbs to help you remember the value of watching your words:

- When words are many, transgression is not lacking, but whoever restrains his lips is prudent. (Proverbs 10:19 ESV)
- Those who guard their lips preserve their lives, but those who speak rashly will come to ruin. (Proverbs 13:3 NIV)
- Whoso keepeth his mouth and his tongue keepeth his soul from troubles. (Proverbs 21:23 KJV)
- There is more hope for a fool than for someone who speaks without thinking. (Proverbs 29:20 NLT)

Words That Matter

If I speak in the tongues of men or of angels,
but do not have love, I am only a resounding
gong or a clanging cymbal.
1 Corinthians 13:1 niv

No matter what we say or how we say it,
if we don't speak in love, then our words are
meaningless—a "resounding gong or a clanging
cymbal," just a bunch of noise. As women who
strive for inner beauty, do we want what we say
to be simply noise filling the air? Or do we want
our words to matter, to have a positive impact, to
mean something to others? If we do, then they
must be spoken with sincere love behind them.

If we talk just to hear our own voices,
then what good is it? If we just brag about our
accomplishments to make ourselves feel better
about ourselves, then what good is it? If we only
yell at our children to get them to listen rather

than lovingly explain why they need to obey, then what good is it? Every conversation we have, every story and experience we share, every joke we tell, every new thing we try to teach our children or say to instruct or discipline them. . .these all can be spoken with sincere love, if we will let our heavenly Father who *is* love (1 John 4:8) help us. And we simply need to ask Him.

The best way we can speak in love is by sharing the Gospel of Jesus Christ with others. Does that mean we randomly shout out scriptures at others, anytime, anywhere? No, we prayerfully seek out opportunities to tell others, in a loving way, about Christ and to encourage them with truth from God's Word. And as the old saying goes, actions speak louder than words. Often what we do to *show* the Gospel of Christ has a much greater effect than what we say about it.

As beautiful women of God, we need to be sure our actions match our words, and both need to be compelled by love.

God has given us two ears, but one tongue, to show that we should be swift to hear, but slow to speak.

THOMAS WATSON

Beautiful Ears,
Listening for God

Being Still

Be still before the LORD.
PSALM 37:7 NIV

It's kind of funny to think about, but short of plastic surgery, there's not much a woman can do physically to her ears to make them more beautiful. They're on the sides of the head and easily covered up with long hair by women who think theirs stick out too much or have a funny shape. Of course it's pretty common for women to pierce their ears in order to wear pretty earrings, but many women choose not to. Whatever the case of the physical appearance of our ears, God doesn't care what they look like on the outside. He cares what they are listening to, and a woman of God will be listening first of all to hear His voice and His leading.

Most women are excellent multitaskers. It's just a trait we have that our ears and brains can easily handle having several things going on at once. But at times, no matter how difficult, we need to turn off multitask mode and simply focus on God. In Psalm 46:10 (NIV) He says, "Be still, and know that I am God."

In other words, we need to be quiet, turn off the TV, radio, and computer, and get away for a few moments of silence and think about who God is and seek Him out in His Word. So many of our concerns and struggles each day can be helped when we just stop to spend some quiet moments listening for and meditating on only God and His greatness, His love and concern for us, and His unending ability to care for us.

We make our ears more beautiful by what we listen to, and the most beautiful ears are those that listen for God.

Plugged In

Let us not neglect our meeting together.
HEBREWS 10:25 NLT

The fact that there is such an incredible amount of media so readily available in this twenty-first century can be a hindrance in listening for God, but it can also be a huge help if we use it wisely. We have access to the Bible like never before, on our computers and tablets and smartphones, through social media, and by downloading sermons and blog posts from great Bible teachers and church leaders in just seconds. But too much can be overwhelming and ineffective, especially if we're not *sincerely* listening but only using it as background noise.

No matter how cool it is and how easily we can bring church into our home through modern technology, it's still best to stay plugged into the Church by joining a Bible-believing church under the authority of a pastor who has been called by God to preach and teach His Word (Hebrews 13; 1 Timothy 5). By attending church regularly and being involved in ministry, we can hear God speak to us through what we do in our churches—listening to teaching, having fellowship with other believers, serving others, and reaching out to those who need the Savior.

Beautiful women of God will use their ears to listen for God in the church under the teaching of a good pastor and in fellowship with other believers because the Bible says, "Let us consider how we may spur one another on toward love and good deeds, not giving up meeting together, as some are in the habit of doing, but encouraging one another—and all the more as you see the Day approaching" (Hebrews 10:24–25 NIV).

Listening and Doing

Listen, you women, to the words of the LORD;
open your ears to what he has to say.
JEREMIAH 9:20 NLT

We all know the saying "It went in one ear and out the other." We're all guilty of hearing without really listening. Yet none of us like it when we're the one not being listened to! If we are to be beautiful in the eyes of the Lord, we need to know when to listen sincerely and connect our ears to our minds and then to our mouths, hearts, hands, and/or feet, depending on how we need to respond.

Especially when it comes to God's Word, we cannot just let it go in one ear and out the other. We should not be just sitting in church on Sunday mornings singing and hearing but not listening, applying, obeying, maturing, and doing. When we read God's Word, it should not just be a quick task to check off our to-do list; we should be encouraged, changed, convicted, taught, and motivated by it.

James 1:22–25 (NIV) says, "Do not merely listen to the word, and so deceive yourselves. Do what it says. Anyone who listens to the word but does not do what it says is like someone who looks at his face in a mirror and, after looking at himself, goes away and immediately forgets what he looks like. But whoever looks intently into the perfect law that gives freedom, and continues in it—not forgetting what they have heard, but doing it—they will be blessed in what they do."

Beautiful ears are not those that hear and then forget. Beautiful ears hear, listen, and then respond in love.

Testing Everything

Test everything that is said. Hold on to what is good.
1 Thessalonians 5:21 NLT

In a world with so much information, it's hard to know what to believe these days. That's why a beautiful woman of God will filter everything she hears through the truth of God's Word.

Since the beginning in the Garden of Eden, an enemy has been trying to deceive us and lead us away from God in every way that he can (Genesis 3; 2 Corinthians 11:3). And the Bible teaches there will be false teachers trying to lead us astray. Consider 2 Peter 2:1–3 (NIV), which says, "But there were also false prophets among the people, just as there will be false teachers among you. . . . Many will follow their depraved conduct and will bring the way of truth into disrepute. In their greed these teachers will exploit you with fabricated stories."

With so much working against us, how can a woman of God truly listen for God's voice among all the noise and deception? By asking God for wisdom and trusting that He will give it. Proverbs 2:1–8 (NLT) says:

> My child, listen to what I say,
>   and treasure my commands.
> Tune your ears to wisdom,
>   and concentrate on understanding.
> Cry out for insight,
>   and ask for understanding.
> Search for them as you would for silver;
>   seek them like hidden treasures.
> Then you will understand what it means
>   to fear the LORD, and you will gain
>   knowledge of God.
> For the LORD grants wisdom!
> From his mouth come knowledge and
>   understanding.
> He grants a treasure of common sense to the
>   honest.
> He is a shield to those who walk with integrity.
> He guards the paths of the just
> and protects those who are faithful to him.

Tuning Out

Whatever is true, whatever is noble, whatever is right, whatever is pure, whatever is lovely, whatever is admirable—if anything is excellent or praiseworthy— think about such things.

PHILIPPIANS 4:8 NIV

*A*my Carmichael was a famous Christian missionary to India who once said, "If I can enjoy a joke at the expense of another; if I can in any way slight another in conversation, or even in thought, then I know nothing of Calvary love." Those are such humbling words because we are all guilty of enjoying jokes at another's expense and slighting others in conversation. It's hard to avoid this type of sin because it's all around us and so easy to participate in. But a beautiful woman of God will do her best to stay away from unwholesome conversation, cruel and crude joking, and foul language.

Of course there are times we simply can't avoid hearing unwholesome talk, and of course there are people we need to minister to who don't know any better. We don't have to live in a protected bubble, speaking and hearing only "Christianese," but we can do our best to turn conversations to positive topics and lovingly ask others to speak kindly in our presence. Sometimes just that simple testimony is enough to help others improve their language and conversation topics, too. And we can always control what we hear in our homes with our choices in music, TV, and movies.

Ears that are constantly full of crude and crass talk will never be able to hear God's voice. Beautiful ears will tune out the negative in this world and tune in to our heavenly Father. Remember what the apostle Paul said: "Whatever is true, whatever is honorable, whatever is just, whatever is pure, whatever is lovely, whatever is commendable, if there is any excellence, if there is anything worthy of praise, think about these things. What you have learned and received and heard and seen in me—practice these things, and the God of peace will be with you" (Philippians 4:8–9 ESV).

Listening with Love

The ears of those who hear will listen.
Isaiah 32:3 NKJV

*W*e all just need a listening ear at times. Someone to hear us out and let us vent our frustrations or to offer a shoulder to cry on. A beautiful woman of God can be that listening ear for others, too, as a way of sharing Christ's love. Sometimes the only good that comes out of our painful experiences is that we in turn can comfort others. If we never go through hard times ourselves, we can't possibly empathize with people who are struggling; we can't listen with understanding and help lead them to the peace that comes only from Jesus.

2 Corinthians 1:5–7 (NIV) says, "For just as we share abundantly in the sufferings of Christ, so also our comfort abounds through Christ. If we are distressed, it is for your comfort and salvation;

if we are comforted, it is for your comfort, which produces in you patient endurance of the same sufferings we suffer. And our hope for you is firm, because we know that just as you share in our sufferings, so also you share in our comfort."

Children especially need our listening ears. Even when their childish needs and struggles seem insignificant compared to grown-up problems, we need to take time to listen intently and let them know that we care and we will help. Jesus Himself said, "Let the little children come to me and do not hinder them, for to such belongs the kingdom of heaven" (Matthew 19:14 ESV). If Jesus took the time to listen to children, then we certainly should, too!

No matter how busy we are with our own problems, women who are beautiful in the eyes of the Lord will take time to be the listening ear that so many people (of all ages!) need.

Listening Like Sheep

My sheep hear my voice.
JOHN 10:27 KJV

❧

It's never wise to compare a woman to a farm animal. However, the Bible means no offense when it talks about Jesus as the Shepherd and us as His sheep. In fact, one of the most beautiful and beloved passages of the Bible is Psalm 23 (NKJV):

> The Lord is my shepherd;
> I shall not want.
> He makes me to lie down in green pastures;
> He leads me beside the still waters.
> He restores my soul;
> He leads me in the paths of righteousness
> For His name's sake.
> Yea, though I walk through the valley of
>   the shadow of death,
> I will fear no evil;

For You are with me;
Your rod and Your staff, they comfort me.
You prepare a table before me in the presence
     of my enemies;
You anoint my head with oil;
My cup runs over.
Surely goodness and mercy shall follow me
All the days of my life;
And I will dwell in the house of the Lord
Forever.

As amusing as it may sound, beautiful women of God will have ears like sheep, listening for the Shepherd. Not because we are dumb or degraded, but because God cares for us like a loving and gentle Shepherd who knows much better than we do the best way that we should go. John 10:27–28 (ESV) says, "My sheep hear my voice, and I know them, and they follow me. I give them eternal life, and they will never perish, and no one will snatch them out of my hand."

What comfort and peace are found in these two different passages of scripture! Jesus our Shepherd leads; we follow, and we can trust Him completely!

Listen and Learn

If you ignore criticism, you will end in poverty and disgrace; if you accept correction, you will be honored.
PROVERBS 13:18 NLT

Who really loves criticism? We like to be encouraged and complimented, not told how we are failing or lacking. Of course we shouldn't enjoy insults, but we can choose to welcome constructive criticism. As godly women we should be humble, admitting there is always something new we can learn, always a way to do better. No matter our education level or area of expertise, we should remain teachable, respecting those who are more mature and experienced and not letting our pride stop us from learning to improve—whether at work, while serving in the church or community, or in our households and our relationships.

We don't have to become doormats, but we

can lovingly show humility, gracefully listening to whatever criticism might come our way, not just instantly putting up our defenses, ready to argue. Then we can pray for discernment and ask God to help us change and grow in light of the criticism, or reject it if it's simply not true—because yes, there will be "Negative Nellies" in our lives who find fault with everything and everybody.

We also have to be careful that we don't surround ourselves only with people who compliment us, constantly stroking our pride and telling us what our itching ears want to hear (2 Timothy 4:3–4). We need family and friends, pastors and leaders in our lives to keep us accountable, to teach us, and to lovingly criticize us at times in order to sharpen us, for the Bible says, "As iron sharpens iron, so one person sharpens another" (Proverbs 27:17 NIV).

A beautiful woman of God uses her ears to wisely discern and accept criticism, choosing not to be defeated or angered by it, knowing it ultimately leads to her honor (Proverbs 13:18).

Always Perked

---

*Blessed is the man who listens to me, watching daily
at my gates, waiting at the posts of my doors.*
PROVERBS 8:34 NKJV

The best way for us to listen for God is to study
His Word and spend quiet time in prayer with
Him. He can also speak to us through others,
through our circumstances, and through creation,
to name just a few other ways. There is really no
way God cannot speak to us if He chooses, for
nothing is impossible with Him (Luke 1:37)!

He spoke to Moses through a burning bush:
"There the angel of the LORD appeared to him
in flames of fire from within a bush. Moses saw
that though the bush was on fire it did not burn
up. So Moses thought, 'I will go over and see
this strange sight—why the bush does not burn
up.' When the LORD saw that he had gone over
to look, God called to him from within the bush,

'Moses! Moses!' " (Exodus 3:2–4 NIV).

He spoke to Mary through the angel Gabriel: "God sent the angel Gabriel to Nazareth, a town in Galilee, to a virgin pledged to be married to a man named Joseph, a descendant of David. The virgin's name was Mary. The angel went to her and said, 'Greetings, you who are highly favored! The Lord is with you' " (Luke 1:26–28 NIV).

He spoke to Saul in a blinding light from heaven on the road to Damascus: "As he neared Damascus on his journey, suddenly a light from heaven flashed around him. He fell to the ground and heard a voice say to him, 'Saul, Saul, why do you persecute me?' " (Acts 9:3–4 NIV).

We might never hear God in such dramatic ways, but He is certainly capable of doing so! And our ears should always be perked, both literally and figuratively, listening for Him to speak, knowing He can and He will when we're eagerly tuned in to Him.

*If you have no joy, there's a leak
in your Christianity somewhere.*

BILLY SUNDAY

A Beautiful Face,
Radiant with Joy

More Than Just Happy

I will greatly rejoice in the LORD,
my soul shall be joyful in my God.
ISAIAH 61:10 KJV

❧

There are far too many things some women
try to make their faces more beautiful—from
moisturizer to makeup to antiwrinkle serums
to the extreme measures of plastic surgery and
Botox injections. Magazines and makeover shows
are constantly sharing ways to try to improve our
faces, make them more beautiful. And yet what
good do all the creams and powders do if there
is never a smile of real joy? A beautiful woman
of God has a face that is *radiant* with joy—not
just happiness, but real joy, which comes only
from knowing Jesus Christ the Savior because
He has reconciled us to God and brought us
into relationship with Him. Romans 5:8–11 (ESV)
describes the source of our joy like this: "But

God shows his love for us in that while we were still sinners, Christ died for us. Since, therefore, we have now been justified by his blood, much more shall we be saved by him from the wrath of God. For if while we were enemies we were reconciled to God by the death of his Son, much more, now that we are reconciled, shall we be saved by his life. More than that, we also rejoice in God through our Lord Jesus Christ, through whom we have now received reconciliation."

Happiness is temporary and fickle, but real joy cannot be changed by circumstances; it is a constant peace and hope and purpose and delight in knowing who we are and that we are *His*. As D. L. Moody wisely put it, "Happiness is caused by things that happen around me, and circumstances will mar it; but joy flows right on through trouble; joy flows on through the dark; joy flows in the night as well as in the day; joy flows all through persecution and opposition."

A woman of God has a face that shines with the radiant joy of Jesus.

Joy in Jesus

Delight yourself in the LORD,
and he will give you the desires of your heart.
PSALM 37:4 ESV

A beautiful woman of God has joy in her salvation through Jesus and in Jesus Himself, in being a follower of Him. John Piper says, "Joy in Christ is the deep good feelings in loving Him and believing Him. It's the echo in our emotions—our hearts—of experiencing Christ as precious and experiencing Christ as reliable. It's the deep good feelings of being attracted to Him for who He is and the deep good feelings of being confident in Him for what He will do."

The nice things we enjoy here on earth are just temporary pleasures, but the joy that fills us up as believers in Jesus is eternal. It's not something always seen or felt in the tangible ways we experience earthly pleasure; rather, it's a love and peace in our souls; it's a faith and hope in things unseen, in a Savior who is unseen. First Peter 1:8 (NLT) says, "You love him even though you have never seen him. Though you do not see him now, you trust him; and you rejoice with a glorious, inexpressible joy."

When we delight in the Lord, He gives us the desires of our hearts (Psalm 37:4). That scripture doesn't mean that if we just enjoy attending church and singing worship songs to God, then we'll receive a new home or car or vacation if we want it. No, it means if we are truly delighting in the Lord, then we are *already* receiving the desires of our hearts—because Jesus Himself is the only lasting fulfillment of all our desires. He alone is the only One who will ever satisfy and bring us real and lasting joy.

No Worries

Do not be afraid, land of Judah; be glad and rejoice.
Surely the LORD has done great things!
JOEL 2:21 NIV

It's a medical fact that stress and worry are harmful to us, causing everything from heart problems and weight fluctuation to hair loss and lines and wrinkles. There is nothing beautiful about stress; and if we let it, it can rob us of our joy.

Women are often natural worriers, but as followers of Jesus we are called to cast all our cares on Him because He cares for us (1 Peter 5:7). Read and remember the following scriptures when you're tempted to let the struggles of life overwhelm you and steal the radiance of joy from your face.

- Do not be anxious about anything, but in everything by prayer and supplication with thanksgiving let your requests be made known to God. And the peace of God, which surpasses all understanding, will guard your hearts and your minds in Christ Jesus. (Philippians 4:6–7 ESV)

- "Therefore I tell you, do not worry about your life, what you will eat or drink; or about your body, what you will wear. Is not life more than food, and the body more than clothes? Look at the birds of the air; they do not sow or reap or store away in barns, and yet your heavenly Father feeds them. Are you not much more valuable than they? Can any one of you by worrying add a single hour to your life?" (Matthew 6:25–27 NIV)

- "So don't worry about tomorrow, for tomorrow will bring its own worries. Today's trouble is enough for today." (Matthew 6:34 NLT)

- But my God shall supply all your need according to his riches in glory by Christ Jesus. (Philippians 4:19 KJV)

Relieved

*What joy for those whose record
the LORD has cleared of guilt.*
PSALM 32:2 NLT

*E*ven as we become beautiful women of the Lord, we're still not perfect. We will still mess up each and every day because of our sinful natures. Paul describes it this way in Romans 7:24–25 (NLT): "Oh, what a miserable person I am! Who will free me from this life that is dominated by sin and death? Thank God! The answer is in Jesus Christ our Lord. So you see how it is: In my mind I really want to obey God's law, but because of my sinful nature I am a slave to sin."

With Jesus as our Savior we are ultimately forgiven, but we still sin daily, and the burden of that sin is heavy. We must constantly confess it if we want to be relieved from it. The joy that results is better than any earthly joy.

Psalm 32 (NLT) perhaps best describes the joy from forgiveness of sin:

Oh, what joy for those
whose disobedience is forgiven,
whose sin is put out of sight!
Yes, what joy for those
whose record the LORD has cleared of guilt,
whose lives are lived in complete honesty!
When I refused to confess my sin,
my body wasted away,
and I groaned all day long. . . .
Finally, I confessed all my sins to you
and stopped trying to hide my guilt.
I said to myself, "I will confess my rebellion
     to the LORD."
And you forgave me! All my guilt is gone. . . .
Many sorrows come to the wicked,
but unfailing love surrounds those who trust
     the LORD.
So rejoice in the LORD and be glad, all you
     who obey him!
Shout for joy, all you whose hearts are pure!

Surrounded

The earth is full of the goodness of the LORD.
PSALM 33:5 KJV

Our God is an incredible artist, as seen in the beauty of His creation, women included! And as women of God we should delight in the beauty of His natural creation—things like watching trees transform into their bright, bold colors for fall, seeing a sunset emblazon the sky with reds and pinks and oranges, or smelling the velvety petals of a gorgeous rose. These simple and common, yet amazing, works of God can bring us great joy and wonder in knowing that the same great God who designed them designed us, too. It's mind boggling to think of how He works and creates! And it's impossible for a woman of God not to praise Him for it. Just look up into the sky on a clear, crisp night and recall Isaiah 40:26 (NIV): "Lift up your eyes and look to the heavens: Who created all these? He who brings out the starry host one by one and calls forth each of them by name. Because of his great power and mighty strength, not one of them is missing."

God's beautiful creation is such a tangible testimony of who He is. Romans 1:20 (NIV) says, "For since the creation of the world God's invisible qualities—his eternal power and divine nature—have been clearly seen, being understood from what has been made, so that people are without excuse."

Sometimes we wish God were more tangible to us, that He would stop over for a chat in our living room or give us a call on the phone. But physical evidence of Him is all around us in His creation. We can be assured of His power, His creativity, and His nature through what we see every day in creation. And this proof of our great God should beautifully brighten our faces with real joy!

Songs and Music

Sing to him, sing praises to him;
tell of all his wondrous works!
PSALM 105:2 ESV

$\mathcal{W}$e have access to music everywhere these days
with MP3 players, satellite radio in our vehicles,
stores and businesses playing music constantly
over speakers, and so on. Unfortunately so much
of it is filled with negative, immoral lyrics. Of
course we don't need to live in a bubble and ban
all secular music from ever entering our ears, but
it's wise to be choosy about what we fill our minds
with in musical form.

Thankfully there are many Christian singers
and musicians of all different genres to satisfy
different musical tastes, but more importantly
to honor God in their lyrics, bringing praise
and glory to Him. We should find great joy in
listening to, singing, and participating in music

that worships God and encourages us in our faith. And we can meditate on the psalms of the Bible, which are poems full of praise and prayers to God, many of which were written to be set to music.

Psalm 33:1–3 (NIV) says, "Sing joyfully to the LORD, you righteous; it is fitting for the upright to praise him. Praise the LORD with the harp; make music to him on the ten-stringed lyre. Sing to him a new song; play skillfully, and shout for joy."

And in the New Testament, scriptures like Colossians 3:16–17 (ESV) instruct us in musical worship: "Let the word of Christ dwell in you richly, teaching and admonishing one another in all wisdom, singing psalms and hymns and spiritual songs, with thankfulness in your hearts to God. And whatever you do, in word or deed, do everything in the name of the Lord Jesus, giving thanks to God the Father through him."

Our faces are always beautiful when radiating with joy in sincere worship of God.

Bittersweet Joy

I am filled with comfort.
I am exceedingly joyful in all our tribulation.
2 CORINTHIANS 7:4 NKJV

*C*orrie ten Boom was a hero of the Christian faith during Adolf Hitler's reign of terror. She and her family endured unspeakable horrors in prison and Nazi concentration camps. Yet among her many writings and teachings, she said, "Joy runs deeper than despair." Corrie certainly had every reason to despair, yet she clung to the joy of Jesus and let Him sustain her.

As women of God, we are actually called to find joy in our sufferings. James 1:2 (NIV) says, "Consider it pure joy, my brothers and sisters, whenever you face trials of many kinds." It does seem ridiculous to be happy about our troubles. Why would God ask this of us? James 1:3 (NIV) goes on to answer that question:

"because you know that the testing of your faith produces perseverance." Our struggles end up strengthening our faith and reliance on God; they draw us closer to Him as we lean on Him, and He is where we find our joy.

When Paul was given a struggle that he prayed God would take away, he said, "I was given a thorn in my flesh, a messenger of Satan, to torment me. Three times I pleaded with the Lord to take it away from me. But he said to me, 'My grace is sufficient for you, for my power is made perfect in weakness.' Therefore I will boast all the more gladly about my weaknesses, so that Christ's power may rest on me. That is why, for Christ's sake, I delight in weaknesses, in insults, in hardships, in persecutions, in difficulties. For when I am weak, then I am strong" (2 Corinthians 12:7–10 NIV).

We can be strong and we can even be happy in our hardships, but only in the strength and joy of Christ.

Getting Good Gifts

Every good gift and every perfect gift is from above,
and cometh down from the Father of lights.
JAMES 1:17 KJV

It's so fun to give a very young child a gift, especially when they are in that stage where the actual opening of the gift brings just as much joy (if not more!) as the gift itself. To a young child at Christmas or on birthdays, everything is new and fun, and they are delighted with and thankful for even the simplest of things. Good parents enjoy giving good gifts to their children, and our heavenly Father delights in giving to His children even more. Jesus said in Matthew 7:9–11 (NLT), "You parents—if your children ask for a loaf of bread, do you give them a stone instead? Or if they ask for a fish, do you give them a snake? Of course not! So if you sinful people know how to give good gifts to your children, how much more will your heavenly Father give good gifts to those who ask him."

We should never lose that childlike joy in receiving good gifts from our heavenly Father, and we should never stop asking Him for them. He invites us to! "Keep on asking, and you will receive what you ask for. Keep on seeking, and you will find. Keep on knocking, and the door will be opened to you. For everyone who asks, receives. Everyone who seeks, finds. And to everyone who knocks, the door will be opened" (Luke 11:9–10 NLT).

May our faces always reflect our joy and gratitude, because we know God provides; all good gifts come from Him (James 1:17); and He is "able to do exceeding abundantly above all that we ask or think" (Ephesians 3:20 KJV).

The Little Things

*Work willingly at whatever you do, as though you
were working for the Lord rather than for people.*
COLOSSIANS 3:23 NLT

⊱⊰

The famous nineteenth-century author Robert
Louis Stevenson said, "The best things are
nearest: breath in your nostrils, light in your eyes,
flowers at your feet, duties at your hand, the path
of right just before you. Do not grasp at the stars,
but do life's plain common work as it comes,
certain that daily duties and daily bread are the
sweetest things in life." What a great reminder
to simply be thankful for the daily tasks at hand
and the common (and often taken for granted)
blessings we have. It's so easy to feel burdened by
all the to-dos on our list at work and/or at home.
But if we'd stop to appreciate what we are capable
of doing and think about how we'd miss those
abilities if they were suddenly gone, they might

not seem so burdensome. In fact, we might even find joy in them.

God wants us to do all things for His glory. First Corinthians 10:31 (NIV) says, "So whether you eat or drink or whatever you do, do it all for the glory of God." That includes having a good attitude. How can we bring glory to God in our activities and work if we grumble about them? In fact, the Bible also says, "Do all things without grumbling or disputing, that you may be blameless and innocent, children of God without blemish in the midst of a crooked and twisted generation, among whom you shine as lights in the world" (Philippians 2:14–15 ESV).

We should strive to find joy in each new day and in all the duties that day holds, remembering every morning when we wake, "This is the day that the LORD has made; let us rejoice and be glad in it" (Psalm 118:24 ESV).

Laughter,
the Best Medicine

A glad heart makes a cheerful face.
PROVERBS 15:13 ESV

We've all heard the saying that laughter is the best medicine. The Bible says, "A merry heart doeth good like a medicine: but a broken spirit drieth the bones" (Proverbs 17:22 KJV). Even in the midst of heartbreaking grief, it can feel good to recall a fond and funny memory shared with a loved one who has passed and smile and laugh through the tears. The joy of laughter can lessen our pain, erase despair, and give us hope. Learning to find the humor in all sorts of situations can help ease tension and frustration, letting us relax and lean on God. He wants to fill our lives and make our faces truly beautiful, radiating with His joy.

The following scriptures tell us more about laughter and joy:

- He will yet fill your mouth with laughter, and your lips with shouting. (Job 8:21 ESV)
- I know the LORD is always with me. I will not be shaken, for he is right beside me. No wonder my heart is glad, and I rejoice. My body rests in safety. (Psalm 16:8–9 NLT)
- When the LORD restored the fortunes of Zion, we were like those who dream. Then our mouth was filled with laughter, and our tongue with shouts of joy. (Psalm 126:1–2 ESV)
- Blessed are ye that weep now: for ye shall laugh. (Luke 6:21 KJV)
- "So with you: Now is your time of grief, but I will see you again and you will rejoice, and no one will take away your joy." (John 16:22 NIV)
- Rejoice evermore. (1 Thessalonians 5:16 KJV)

God has given us two hands,
one to receive with and
the other to give with.

BILLY GRAHAM

Beautiful Hands,
Serving with Love

Active Faith

---

*What good is it, dear brothers and sisters, if you say
you have faith but don't show it by your actions?*
JAMES 2:14 NLT

Soft and smooth with well-manicured
nails—that's how our culture would describe
beautiful hands for a woman. There are whole
stores dedicated to selling fragrant creams and
moisturizers and a host of ways to have our nails
painted, whether we do it ourselves at home or
get a professional manicure. But once again, God
is not concerned with the outer appearance of
our hands. Instead He's concerned with what we
do with them, and a beautiful woman of God
uses her hands to serve others with love.

The Bible talks about how our faith is
meaningless if we do not act it out and serve
others. James 2:14–18 (NLT) says, "What good is it,
dear brothers and sisters, if you say you have faith

but don't show it by your actions? Can that kind of faith save anyone? Suppose you see a brother or sister who has no food or clothing, and you say, 'Good-bye and have a good day; stay warm and eat well'—but then you don't give that person any food or clothing. What good does that do? So you see, faith by itself isn't enough. Unless it produces good deeds, it is dead and useless. Now someone may argue, 'Some people have faith; others have good deeds.' But I say, 'How can you show me your faith if you don't have good deeds? I will show you my faith by my good deeds.' "

Our hands are truly beautiful when they are actively showing our faith through our good deeds.

Serving the King

———— ❧ ————

"The King will reply, 'Truly I tell you,
whatever you did for one of the least of these
brothers and sisters of mine, you did for me.' "
MATTHEW 25:40 NIV

———— ❧ ————

There are so many types of nonprofit
organizations and ministries, all of which seem
to be doing good work to help people. How do
we know which ones are worthy of our service
and support? Jesus talks about serving others in
Matthew 25:35–40 (NIV); He says, " 'For I was
hungry and you gave me something to eat, I was
thirsty and you gave me something to drink, I
was a stranger and you invited me in, I needed
clothes and you clothed me, I was sick and you
looked after me, I was in prison and you came
to visit me.' Then the righteous will answer him,
'Lord, when did we see you hungry and feed you,
or thirsty and give you something to drink? When

did we see you a stranger and invite you in, or needing clothes and clothe you? When did we see you sick or in prison and go to visit you?' The King will reply, 'Truly I tell you, whatever you did for one of the least of these brothers and sisters of mine, you did for me.' "

Our hands are beautiful when they care for and provide for others who are in need in Jesus' name. It's amazing to think that He says when we do so, it's the same as serving Jesus Himself. What an honor to serve the King of kings!

Special Guests

---

*If you help the poor, you are lending to
the LORD—and he will repay you!*
PROVERBS 19:17 NLT

A beautiful, poetic portrayal of the scriptures,
Helen Steiner Rice's poem "The Christmas
Guest," featuring Matthew 25:35–40, has been
recorded by several country artists including
Grandpa Jones, Johnny Cash, and Reba McEntire.
In it, an old man is waiting expectantly on
Christmas Eve for the Lord to come to his home
because the Lord told him in a dream that He
would visit him as his Christmas guest. However,
when Christmas Day comes to an end, Conrad
is disappointed because his only visitors were a
poor beggar with no shoes (Conrad invited him in
and gave him shoes and a coat), an elderly woman
who needed to rest (Conrad invited her in for a
warm drink), and a lost little girl who needed to

find her family (Conrad helped her). Conrad cries out to God, wondering why He didn't come like He promised.

And then Conrad is humbled by God's voice saying, "Lift up your head, for I kept my word," and explaining how He was the beggar, the old woman, and the little girl, and each thing that Conrad had done for these people in need, he had done for Jesus.

If only we can strive to remember every moment of every day, even when we feel we have nothing to give, that our service to others, our generosity and caring and providing with our hands and hearts and all our resources, is actually done to Jesus Himself, what better attitudes we would have and what incredible and beautiful testimonies our lives would be!

Happy Hands

Do not neglect to do good and to share what you have,
for such sacrifices are pleasing to God.
HEBREWS 13:16 ESV

Beautiful hands are gentle when caring and providing for others and cheerful in all their tasks. What love or tenderness is there in yanking a child along when we could gently hold his hand to guide him? Or in slamming dishes around in the kitchen when we're frustrated with all the housework that needs to be done? Even when we are tired, frustrated, angry, or all of the above (sometimes rightfully so!), we can ask God to help us choose to be gentle and kind even though we don't feel like it. In our selfish human nature, we might not be able to muster the gentleness needed, but God is in us through His Holy Spirit and we can ask Him for help. "For God is working in you, giving you the desire and the power to do what pleases him" (Philippians 2:13 NLT).

As we go about our tasks, we should be cheerful, not begrudging them. "Do everything without complaining and arguing, so that no one can criticize you. Live clean, innocent lives as children of God, shining like bright lights in a world full of crooked and perverse people" (Philippians 2:14–15 NLT).

It is not just that we use our hands to serve others that matters; it is also the *way* we use them while we serve. Hands that give to others with gentleness and with a happy heart are what God finds beautiful, because "God loves a cheerful giver" (2 Corinthians 9:7 NIV).

Warm and Welcoming

Seek to show hospitality.
ROMANS 12:13 ESV

The beautiful hands of a woman of God are welcoming when greeting and ushering guests into her home. It's called hospitality, and God encourages us in His Word to practice hospitality to others. Consider these scriptures:

- Don't forget to show hospitality to strangers, for some who have done this have entertained angels without realizing it! (Hebrews 13:2 NLT)
- Offer hospitality to one another without grumbling. (1 Peter 4:9 NIV)
- Contribute to the needs of the saints and seek to show hospitality. (Romans 12:13 ESV)
- "If anyone gives you even a cup of water because you belong to the Messiah, I tell

you the truth, that person will surely be rewarded." (Mark 9:41 NLT)

Hospitality does not mean that you can only open your home to others when you've invited them over and the house is spotless. We need to be willing to accept guests at all times, even unexpected times, for that is true hospitality. We can strive to keep our homes neat and appealing according to whatever standards of "clean" we're comfortable with, but they don't always have to be immaculate, and we don't always have to have a gourmet meal or a snack tray ready. Just a glass of ice water or cup of tea or coffee can be more than enough, because what matters is a kind and welcoming attitude, a listening ear, and a loving heart. The key to hospitality is balancing the attitudes of Martha and Mary in Luke 10:38–41. Martha kindly invited Jesus into her home but became too preoccupied with the chores and details of hosting a guest, while Mary chose to take time to simply listen to Jesus.

Held

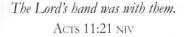

The Lord's hand was with them.
Acts 11:21 NIV

*H*ands that are truly beautiful are ones that are
constantly held and led by God's hand. The song
"Held" recorded by Christian artist Natalie Grant
is a stirring reminder of this—that no matter
what we are going through in life, no matter
how painful it is or what is torn from us, we will
survive it because God will never stop holding us
through it.

Isaiah 41:10 (NIV) says, "So do not fear, for I
am with you; do not be dismayed, for I am your
God. I will strengthen you and help you; I will
uphold you with my righteous right hand."

God's hands are powerful, delivering judgment
and wrath at times (1 Samuel 5:6; Matthew 21:12)
or calming a storm (Mark 4:35–41), but they are
also gentle and loving, like when Jesus laid His

hands on the little children (Matthew 19:13–15) or healed the sick (Mark 8:25; 9:27). His hands are always exactly what we need, when we need it. A strong grip to keep us from falling, a gentle caress to wipe away a tear, a guiding gesture to show us the right way. And He uses His people here on earth, our fellow brothers and sisters in Christ, to be His hands to us. He also uses His angels. Hebrews 1:14 (ESV) says about them, "Are they not all ministering spirits sent out to serve for the sake of those who are to inherit salvation?"

No matter our circumstances, whether good or bad, as beautiful women of God, we are immeasurably blessed to be constantly held by His almighty, loving hand.

Comforting

---

*Now may our Lord Jesus Christ himself,
and God our Father, who loved us and gave us eternal
comfort and good hope through grace, comfort your hearts
and establish them in every good work and word.*
2 Thessalonians 2:16–17 esv

With our hands, we can offer comfort; sometimes better than any word is just the squeeze of a hand or a loving pat on the back or the stroke of a cheek. Especially with someone who is sick or dying or with an elderly person whose mind is failing, though communication with spoken words might be difficult, a tender touch speaks volumes.

Babies and young children are also comforted and loved by our hands. Before babies can talk, their mothers' hands show love by holding them, bathing them, feeding them, and caring for them in every way. Toddlers who are still trying to learn to put emotions into words will benefit from parents who comfort them during tears and tantrums.

Isaiah 40 (NIV) is a beautiful passage of scripture that begins, "Comfort, comfort my people, says your God," and ends with some of the most comforting verses in the Bible, especially for anyone suffering or struggling who needs strength:

> The LORD is the everlasting God,
> the Creator of the ends of the earth.
> He will not grow tired or weary,
> and his understanding no one can fathom.
> He gives strength to the weary
> and increases the power of the weak.
> Even youths grow tired and weary,
> and young men stumble and fall;
> but those who hope in the LORD
> will renew their strength.
> They will soar on wings like eagles;
> they will run and not grow weary,
> they will walk and not be faint. (verses 28–31)

God is our ultimate and best Comforter, and if our hands are truly beautiful they will seek to share that comfort with others.

Folded in Prayer

Every day I call upon you, O LORD;
I spread out my hands to you.
PSALM 88:9 ESV

It's certainly not necessary to fold our hands in prayer; we can talk to God in any way at any time. But folding hands for prayer is a practice many teach to children at a young age (in part to help them keep still and quiet!), so folded hands are a common symbol of prayer. Whether literally or figuratively, hands that are frequently folded in prayer are truly beautiful because a beautiful woman of God is in continuous conversation with her heavenly Father. The Bible instructs us to "pray without ceasing" (1 Thessalonians 5:17 ESV).

A woman of God prays for more and more opportunities to serve others with her hands and with her love. She prays for God to help her keep her eyes open and her ears attentive to what those around her might need. She looks for ways to be a testimony with her hands, doing things in Jesus' name in such a way that others who don't know the Savior are appreciative of and intrigued, that she might draw them to the Gospel.

We are beautiful to God when we pray for wisdom—for opportunities and the desire to give and serve discreetly, not needing to brag or promote ourselves for our charity, and knowing that our real rewards are in heaven and not here on earth. Matthew 6:1–4 (NLT) says, "Watch out! Don't do your good deeds publicly, to be admired by others, for you will lose the reward from your Father in heaven. When you give to someone in need, don't do as the hypocrites do—blowing trumpets in the synagogues and streets to call attention to their acts of charity! I tell you the truth, they have received all the reward they will ever get. But when you give to someone in need, don't let your left hand know what your right hand is doing. Give your gifts in private, and your Father, who sees everything, will reward you."

Busy Hands

Honor her for all that her hands have done.
PROVERBS 31:31 NIV

The wife of noble character described in Proverbs 31 is certainly a beautiful woman of God and a very busy lady! Her hands are rarely idle. Consider all the ways she uses her hands:

She selects wool and flax and works with eager hands. (31:13)

She is like the merchant ships, bringing her food from afar. (31:14)

She gets up while it is still night; she provides food for her family and portions for her female servants. (31:15)

She sets about her work vigorously; her arms are strong for her tasks. (31:17)

She holds the distaff and grasps the spindle with her fingers. (31:19)

She opens her arms to the poor and extends her hands to the needy. (31:20)

She makes coverings for her bed; she is clothed in fine linen and purple. (31:22)

She makes linen garments and sells them, and supplies the merchants with sashes. (31:24)

Obviously in our culture today, we don't do things exactly as the Proverbs 31 woman needed to, and we all have different physical abilities as well. The point is, she can inspire us! We can apply her character to our own lives and actions, especially that she is never lazy. She constantly seeks to serve and support her husband, her family, and those around her. Of course, she needs time to rest, too. This passage of scripture is not intended to work us to the bone, but it shows the many accomplishments a woman of God is capable of when she honors Him with her duties and draws her strength and motivation from Him. The passage finishes up with, "Charm is deceptive, and beauty is fleeting; but a woman who fears the LORD is to be praised. Honor her for all that her hands have done, and let her works bring her praise at the city gate."

Not Afraid to Let Go

*Love not the world,
neither the things that are in the world.*
1 JOHN 2:15 KJV

When it comes to our possessions, we are often like babies who have just learned to grasp on to something. We don't want to let go! Often it took a lot of hard work to get our money, our homes, our vehicles, our toys. But if we never let go of what we have, we won't be open to the new blessings God has for us. Augustine put it wisely: "God is always trying to give good things to us, but our hands are too full to receive them."

Sometimes a child who won't let go of the toys in her hands is missing out on the special treat her mother wants to place there instead. It's the same with us and our heavenly Father. Sometimes we can't receive the new gift He has for us because we don't want to let go of the old. This applies to our possessions, our dreams, our relationships. . .*everything* in our lives. The Christian life is about giving up everything so that we can gain even more. Jesus said, "If anyone desires to come after Me, let him deny himself, and take up his cross, and follow Me. For whoever desires to save his life will lose it, but whoever loses his life for My sake will find it. For what profit is it to a man if he gains the whole world, and loses his own soul? Or what will a man give in exchange for his soul? For the Son of Man will come in the glory of His Father with His angels, and then He will reward each according to his works" (Matthew 16:24–27 NKJV).

A beautiful woman of God does not stubbornly hold on to the things of this world. She gives up her own life in order to gain the truly beautiful one God has in store for her.

Every path that leads to heaven
is trodden by willing feet.
No one is ever driven to paradise.

HOWARD CROSBY

Beautiful Feet,
Following God

Lovingly Led

Teach me to do your will, for you are my God!
Let your good Spirit lead me on level ground!
PSALM 143:10 ESV

To have truly beautiful feet, it doesn't matter
what shoes or socks or hosiery you're wearing
or what color your toes might be painted. No
amount of pedicures or pretty polish really
matters. What matters is who you're following,
whose path you're walking in. And a woman
who is lovely to God follows after her Lord and
Savior.

Every day she should ask Him to lead her
in His ways, to direct her steps where He would
have her go, to guide her according to His will, to
reveal His plans for her. Memorize, meditate on,
and pray scriptures like these from Psalms and
Proverbs as you follow hard after God:

- Lead me, O LORD, in thy righteousness because of mine enemies; make thy way straight before my face. (Psalm 5:8 KJV)

- The LORD says, "I will guide you along the best pathway for your life. I will advise you and watch over you." (Psalm 32:8 NLT)

- Search me, God, and know my heart; test me and know my anxious thoughts. See if there is any offensive way in me, and lead me in the way everlasting. (Psalm 139:23–24 NIV)

- You hold me by my right hand. You will guide me with Your counsel, and afterward receive me to glory. (Psalm 73:23–24 NKJV)

- Trust in the LORD with all thine heart; and lean not unto thine own understanding. In all thy ways acknowledge him, and he shall direct thy paths. (Proverbs 3:5–6 KJV)

- The heart of man plans his way, but the LORD establishes his steps. (Proverbs 16:9 ESV)

No Need to Brag

Do not boast about tomorrow,
for you do not know what a day may bring forth.
PROVERBS 27:1 NKJV

We probably all know people who love to brag about what they plan to do, and hearing them go on and on about all their accomplishments or possessions or big plans for the future can get old fast. John Piper said it well: "Boasting is the outward form of the inner condition of pride." Of course we should encourage and support others, but there's a difference between people who humbly work hard toward good goals and people who do more bragging and boasting about what they plan to accomplish than actually working toward it.

James warns against boasting about the future, saying, "Now listen, you who say, 'Today or tomorrow we will go to this or that city, spend

a year there, carry on business and make money.'
Why, you do not even know what will happen
tomorrow. What is your life? You are a mist
that appears for a little while and then vanishes.
Instead, you ought to say, 'If it is the Lord's will,
we will live and do this or that.' As it is, you boast
in your arrogant schemes. All such boasting is
evil" (James 4:13–16 NIV).

Beautiful feet follow after God. We don't
need to boast in any plans of our own. Only God
holds the future and knows how many moments
we have here on earth. Rather than boasting in
ourselves or others, we should boast in the Lord
alone; as 2 Corinthians 10:17 (ESV) says, "Let the
one who boasts, boast in the Lord."

When the Going Gets Tough

All of your works will thank you, Lord,
and your faithful followers will praise you.
PSALM 145:10 NLT

Just like the old saying, "When the going gets tough, the tough get going," a beautiful woman of God follows after Him even when the way is hard. The world often mocks Christians for staying committed to Christ even in the midst of great suffering. Job's wife gave the prime example of this when she looked at his suffering and said, "Do you still hold fast your integrity? Curse God and die" (Job 2:9 ESV).

Never take the advice of Job's wife. We should follow God no matter how hard things get. But the way won't be easy. Jesus Himself said, "You can enter God's Kingdom only through the narrow gate. The highway to hell is broad, and its gate is wide for the many who choose that way. But the gateway to life is very narrow and the road is difficult, and only a few ever find it" (Matthew 7:13–14 NLT).

We should expect to share in Christ's sufferings (Philippians 3:10–11), but we will be comforted and strengthened through them. "For the more we suffer for Christ, the more God will shower us with his comfort through Christ" (2 Corinthians 1:5 NLT). And we can say like Paul, "I take pleasure in my weaknesses, and in the insults, hardships, persecutions, and troubles that I suffer for Christ. For when I am weak, then I am strong" (2 Corinthians 12:10 NLT). Because in our weakness God gives us His strength.

A beautiful woman of God has feet that follow Him faithfully as she trusts that His Word and His promises are true, and that His way, no matter how hard, is always better.

Following the Great Commission

That is why the Scriptures say, "How beautiful are the feet of messengers who bring good news!"
ROMANS 10:15 NLT

The Gospel of Matthew ends with the resurrected Jesus speaking to the eleven disciples in what is called the Great Commission: "And Jesus came and spoke to them, saying, 'All authority has been given to Me in heaven and on earth. Go therefore and make disciples of all the nations, baptizing them in the name of the Father and of the Son and of the Holy Spirit, teaching them to observe all things that I have commanded you; and lo, I am with you always, even to the end of the age.' Amen" (Matthew 28:18–20 NKJV).

We also must follow the Great Commission, telling others about Jesus, seeking to help them know Him like we do—that He is our only hope for salvation. Paul says in Romans, " 'Everyone who calls on the name of the LORD will be saved.' But how can they call on him to save them unless they believe in him? And how can they believe in him if they have never heard about him? And how can they hear about him unless someone tells them? And how will anyone go and tell them without being sent? That is why the Scriptures say, 'How beautiful are the feet of messengers who bring good news!' " (Romans 10:13–15 NLT).

Our feet are truly beautiful by bringing the Good News, the Gospel of Christ, to others, whether in a foreign country or simply in our neighborhoods and workplaces and activities. Jesus is needed everywhere, and it's our job to be on our feet, taking Him everywhere and making Him known.

How to Follow the Great Commission

God has given us different gifts for doing certain things well.

ROMANS 12:6 NLT

Following the Great Commission does not mean we all have to pack up and head to a foreign country as missionaries. Not everyone is called to be an overseas missionary or pastor or church leader. But we are all called to use our spiritual gifts. Paul says in Romans 12:6–8 (NLT), "In his grace, God has given us different gifts for doing certain things well. So if God has given you the ability to prophesy, speak out with as much faith as God has given you. If your gift is serving others, serve them well. If you are a teacher, teach well. If your gift is to encourage others, be encouraging. If it is giving, give generously.

If God has given you leadership ability, take the responsibility seriously. And if you have a gift for showing kindness to others, do it gladly." And in 1 Corinthians 12, Paul talks about how we are all part of the body of Christ with different gifts, none of which is more or less important than any other. We are all needed to fulfill His purposes. We follow the Great Commission of bringing others to Christ by being active in the body of Christ, using our gifts to reach out to others and share the Good News.

A beautiful woman of God doesn't have to be involved in every ministry opportunity available; she prays for wisdom to realize her spiritual gifts and direction to know where God best wants her to use them in order to share Jesus with those who need to know the Savior.

Being Obedient

Loving God means keeping his commandments.
1 JOHN 5:3 NLT

Those of us who are moms or caretakers of children know that teaching kids obedience is one of the hardest parts of childrearing. Some children are fairly easygoing and compliant. Others seem to fight tooth-and-nail over even the simplest tasks—and cause a new gray hair to sprout each time! Why is it so hard at times for children to learn that when they listen and follow directions and rules, it is for their benefit, to keep them safe, healthy, learning, disciplined, and rewarded?

Our heavenly Father wants us to learn obedience, and He wants to reward us for it, too. First John 5:3–4 (NLT) says, "Loving God means keeping his commandments, and his commandments are not burdensome. For every child of God defeats this evil world, and we achieve this victory through our faith." Keeping God's commands is what helps us overcome the world. Rejecting God and His Word, which is our guidebook for living, will only result in our destruction along with that of the world, but accepting Christ and following Him, obeying Him and His commandments, will result in everlasting life. Consider 1 John 2:16–17 (NLT): "For the world offers only a craving for physical pleasure, a craving for everything we see, and pride in our achievements and possessions. These are not from the Father, but are from this world. And this world is fading away, along with everything that people crave. But anyone who does what pleases God will live forever."

Many people think that Christianity is just another religion with a bunch of rules to follow, one giant killjoy to life, but women who are following Christ know that it is about a relationship with a Savior who wants us to obey Him and follow Him through this world (with victory over it!) and into the place He's preparing for us, which will be a perfect paradise in the presence of God for eternity.

Following God's Greatest Commandments

Master, which is the great commandment in the law?
MATTHEW 22:36 KJV

When we're doing our best to obey God, it's easy to wonder, "Are some of God's commands more important than others? Do we just follow the Ten Commandments of the Old Testament?" Jesus was asked in Matthew 22 which commandment was the greatest. He answered, "You shall love the Lord your God with all your heart and with all your soul and with all your mind. This is the great and first commandment. And a second is like it: You shall love your neighbor as yourself" (Matthew 22:37–39 ESV).

In these two commandments, Jesus summed up exactly how to obey and follow Him. He boiled it down for us, saying, "On these two commandments depend all the Law and the Prophets" (Matthew 22:40 ESV). This clearly shows that the Christian life is *not* about following a huge book of rules and regulations. It's simply about loving God with everything we have—heart, soul, and mind. If we do that, if we truly love God, then we will naturally want to please Him; we will want to study His Word and do our best to keep the rest of His commands for holy living.

And when we follow the second command to love our neighbors as ourselves—not just with kindness and manners, but really loving those around us and seeking to meet their needs just like we take care of ourselves—then we share God's love and attract others to a relationship with Him like we have.

A beautiful woman of God is not overwhelmed by a set of religious rules; she simply does her best to obey the two greatest commandments Jesus gave, knowing that they are the key to being a true follower of Christ.

Getting Uncomfortable

---

*For the Spirit God gave us does not make us timid,
but gives us power, love and self-discipline.*
2 TIMOTHY 1:7 NIV

❧

In our culture, we delight in our comforts.
Comfort foods, comfortable clothes and shoes,
comfortable furniture to relax in, comfortable
cars to drive. But as women who are lovely to
God, we are called to be uncomfortable at times,
too, and not by wearing high heels and pantyhose.

It's not easy to leave our comfort zones. It's
not in our nature to wake up and say, "I'd like to
be uncomfortable today." But God wants us to
follow Him into the unknown, into where He
can use us for His purposes and His glory, and
to trust Him to see us through it. Some women
are natural risk takers who thrive on change
and adventure, but for others it's downright
terrifying to even think about walking across the

street to a neighbors' home to invite them to church. No matter the radius of our circles of comfort, we all need to consider Paul's words to Timothy in 2 Timothy 1:7–10 (NLT): "For God has not given us a spirit of fear and timidity, but of power, love, and self-discipline. So never be ashamed to tell others about our Lord. And don't be ashamed of me, either, even though I'm in prison for him. With the strength God gives you, be ready to suffer with me for the sake of the Good News. For God saved us and called us to live a holy life. He did this, not because we deserved it, but because that was his plan from before the beginning of time—to show us his grace through Christ Jesus. And now he has made all of this plain to us by the appearing of Christ Jesus, our Savior. He broke the power of death and illuminated the way to life and immortality through the Good News."

Following God out of our comfort zones is never without sacrifice, but it is also not without great reward, "for our light and momentary troubles are achieving for us an eternal glory that far outweighs them all" (2 Corinthians 4:17 NIV).

Wait Times

Wait for the LORD and keep his way.
PSALM 37:34 ESV

Anyone who has ever let a small child lead the way on an outdoor walk knows you have to follow with patience sometimes as they stop to examine random rocks, bugs, and leaves along the way. God wants us to follow Him with patience, too. We like for things to happen in our own timing, but our times are in His hands (Psalm 31:15). We wish God would move and answer our prayers immediately, but "a day is like a thousand years to the Lord, and a thousand years is like a day" (2 Peter 3:8 NLT). We wish Jesus would hurry up and return and establish His new and perfect kingdom, but "the Lord isn't really being slow about his promise, as some people think. No, he is being patient for your sake. He does not want anyone to be destroyed, but wants everyone to repent" (2 Peter 3:9 NLT).

God uses our waiting times to teach us and mature us and prepare us for what He has planned next. According to John Ortberg, "Biblically, waiting is not just something we have to do until we get what we want. Waiting is part of the process of becoming what God wants us to be." And sometimes God makes us wait in order to protect us. George MacDonald has said, "He may delay because it would not be safe to give us at once what we ask: we are not ready for it. To give ere we could truly receive would be to destroy the very heart and hope of prayer, to cease to be our Father. The delay itself may work to bring us nearer to our help, to increase the desire, perfect the prayer, and ripen the receptive condition."

A beautiful woman of God lets Him lead, and she follows Him patiently, knowing that His timing is always the best.

You don't have a soul.
You are a Soul.
You have a body.
C. S. LEWIS

A Beautiful Body,
from the Inside Out

Inner Beauty

I praise you, for I am fearfully and wonderfully made.
Wonderful are your works; my soul knows it very well.
PSALM 139:14 ESV

Is there any woman among us who doesn't occasionally complain about at least one feature of her body? We all struggle at times with discontentment over our physical figures. Our culture glamorizes thin and curvy measurements that are nearly impossible for most women to maintain. Having a positive self-image is such a challenge in the world we live in. We will never view our bodies as beautiful if we only compare them to the standards set in our fallen world, standards that seem to be defined solely by sexual immorality.

To see her body as beautiful, a woman of God must remember that He has made her in His image (Genesis 1:27), He knit her together in her mother's womb (Psalm 139:13), and she is fearfully and wonderfully made (Psalm 139:14). We have to choose daily not to compare ourselves with others—celebrities especially!—remembering that we are purposefully created by God, and our bodies were designed specifically and *uniquely* by Him. If we ever start to doubt this, we need to consider how no two fingerprints are exactly the same—amazing!

A positive self-image of our bodies begins with accepting ourselves for who we are, refusing to compare ourselves to others, and then working on keeping our bodies as healthy as possible— not in a way the world demands but in a way that honors our Creator. Most important of all, remember that people may be concerned with our outer appearance, but God looks at the heart. Our bodies should be beautiful from the inside out, as 1 Peter 3:3–4 (NKJV) instructs: "Do not let your adornment be merely outward. . .rather let it be the hidden person of the heart, with the incorruptible beauty of a gentle and quiet spirit, which is very precious in the sight of God."

Temple of God

Do you not know that you are God's temple
and that God's Spirit dwells in you?
1 Corinthians 3:16 esv

As beautiful women of God, we need to
remember that our bodies are not our own. In this
culture of ultra-feminism, that is taken offensively
by some women, but it is certainly not intended
to offend. It means that when we accept Jesus as
Savior, we welcome Him into our lives, letting the
Holy Spirit, whom Jesus said He would send to us
in His absence (John 16:7), dwell in us and do what
Jesus promised He would do: "When the Spirit of
truth comes, he will guide you into all the truth,
for he will not speak on his own authority, but
whatever he hears he will speak, and he will declare
to you the things that are to come. He will glorify
me, for he will take what is mine and declare it to
you. All that the Father has is mine; therefore I said

that he will take what is mine and declare it to you" (John 16:13–15 ESV).

Having the Spirit of God living in us and leading us in all truth sounds like an incredible blessing, not any reason to be offended! In light of this, we're given a responsibility to honor Him by honoring our bodies, protecting them from sin—including overindulging in alcohol and food, misusing drugs, and being sexually immoral. Paul sums it up well in 1 Corinthians 6:19–20 (ESV), asking, "Do you not know that your body is a temple of the Holy Spirit within you, whom you have from God? You are not your own, for you were bought with a price. So glorify God in your body."

A Healthy Diet

"Sir," they said, *"give us that bread every day."*
JOHN 6:34 NLT

---

*O*bviously a woman of God can't keep her body beautiful if her diet is loaded with junk food. To maintain a beautiful physical body and healthy lifestyle, she needs nutritious food and drink. Neither can a woman keep her body beautiful on the inside unless she's feeding her spirit a healthy diet. Jesus said He is our Living Water and our Bread of Life. In John 4:14 (ESV), Jesus tells the Samaritan woman, "Whoever drinks of the water that I will give him will never be thirsty again. The water that I will give him will become in him a spring of water welling up to eternal life."

And in John 6:35–40 (NLT), He says, "I am the bread of life. Whoever comes to me will never be hungry again. Whoever believes in me will never be thirsty. . . . For I have come down from heaven to do the will of God who sent me, not to do my own will. And this is the will of God, that I should not lose even one of all those he has given me, but that I should raise them up at the last day. For it is my Father's will that all who see his Son and believe in him should have eternal life."

So how do we stay on this Jesus diet of Living Water and Bread of Life, this pure nutrition for our souls that will one day result in perfect bodies in heaven? We "live and move and have our being" in Him (Acts 17:28 NIV); we dig into His Word every day; we remain in constant conversation with Him through prayer; we fellowship with other believers and encourage one another in faith; we minister to the needy and help bring them to Jesus; we love Him and seek after Him with everything we are and everything we have and everything we do.

Bearing Fruit

"But the fruit of the Spirit is. . ."
GALATIANS 5:22 ESV

$\mathcal{A}$ woman of God does not follow all the desires of her body. Instead she bears good fruit. That might create a funny image in your mind, but of course it doesn't mean we should literally have apples and oranges and pears growing off of our limbs. It means we exhibit the presence of the Holy Spirit in our lives through what the Bible calls the fruit of the Spirit. In Galatians 5 Paul is comparing how people controlled by the sinful desires of their human bodies end up in all kinds of sin, but people who have accepted Christ are controlled by the Holy Spirit and begin to show the fruit of the Spirit, which is love, joy, peace, patience, kindness, goodness, faithfulness, gentleness, and self-control: "But I say, walk by the Spirit, and you will not gratify the desires of the flesh. . . . Now the works of the flesh are evident: sexual immorality, impurity, sensuality, idolatry, sorcery, enmity, strife, jealousy, fits of anger, rivalries, dissensions, divisions, envy, drunkenness, orgies, and things like these. I warn you, as I warned you before, that those who do such things will not inherit the kingdom of God. But the fruit of the Spirit is love, joy, peace, patience, kindness, goodness, faithfulness, gentleness, self-control; against such things there is no law. And those who belong to Christ Jesus have crucified the flesh with its passions and desires" (Galatians 5:16–24 ESV).

The fruit of the Spirit does not appear instantly in our lives once we've accepted Christ; it's something continuously cultivated by those who desire a beautiful spirit. As Rick Warren has put it, "God develops the fruit of the Spirit in your life by allowing you to experience circumstances in which you're tempted to express the exact opposite quality. Character development always involves a choice, and temptation provides that opportunity."

Protected

—⚬—

Put on every piece of God's armor so you will be
able to resist the enemy in the time of evil.
EPHESIANS 6:13 NLT

⚬

Self-defense classes are an excellent idea for
women to help us protect ourselves in a world
that's unfortunately full of evil. Even if we think
we'd never really be able to fight back, at the
very least, educating ourselves on how to avoid
dangerous situations is important.

Women of God also have greater battles to
consider and thankfully even better protection
than just human self-defense. We have spiritual
battles to face, because "we are not fighting
against flesh-and-blood enemies, but against evil
rulers and authorities of the unseen world, against
mighty powers in this dark world, and against evil
spirits in the heavenly places" (Ephesians 6:12
NLT). Thankfully, though, we have great spiritual

protection because we have constant access to the full armor of God! Paul says in Ephesians 6:13–18 (NLT), "Put on every piece of God's armor so you will be able to resist the enemy in the time of evil. Then after the battle you will still be standing firm. Stand your ground, putting on the belt of truth and the body armor of God's righteousness. For shoes, put on the peace that comes from the Good News so that you will be fully prepared. In addition to all of these, hold up the shield of faith to stop the fiery arrows of the devil. Put on salvation as your helmet, and take the sword of the Spirit, which is the word of God. Pray in the Spirit at all times and on every occasion. Stay alert and be persistent in your prayers for all believers everywhere."

God protects us from sin and spiritual battles with a supernaturally strong suit of armor.

Keeping Pure

Create in me a pure heart, O God.
PSALM 51:10 NIV

"Sex sells" is unfortunately so true in our society, and sexual sin seems to be infiltrating practically everything these days—even children's movies are full of innuendo. It's quite a challenge for a godly woman to follow the teaching of Paul in 1 Thessalonians 4: "God's will is for you to be holy, so stay away from all sexual sin. Then each of you will control his own body and live in holiness and honor—not in lustful passion like the pagans who do not know God and his ways. . . . God has called us to live holy lives, not impure lives" (vv. 3–7 NLT).

We need to watch how we dress, how we act, how we talk and tease, what we watch, read, listen to, and participate in. We should be careful of what we teach younger women and girls, being careful that all our actions, attitudes, and fashion choices reflect a desire to remain sexually pure—because that is God's will for us. Because He's a killjoy? Absolutely not. Because He's the designer of sexuality, and He knows it is beautiful and healthy and a blessing to us only when it is kept pure.

Keeping our bodies sexually pure is not just a concern for young and single women of God. All married Christian women need to constantly guard their hearts against sexual temptation, too. A racy book or two read "just for fun" or a little flirting here and there might seem harmless, yet our enemy is hoping to use these things as footholds to make marriages fail and to destroy our purity. We are to "be alert and of sober mind. Your enemy the devil prowls around like a roaring lion looking for someone to devour. Resist him" (1 Peter 5:8–9 NIV).

As we stay alert and avoid sexual sin, may our prayer as beautiful women of God constantly be, "Create in me a pure heart."

Wonderfully Weak

When I am weak, then I am strong.
2 Corinthians 12:10 niv

People of faith who are strongest are often those lying on their deathbeds, with bodies so weak they can barely take a breath, for God has said, "My grace is sufficient for you, for my power is made perfect in weakness" (2 Corinthians 12:9 esv). They are strong because nothing is left of their body's strength and they have complete reliance on God, depending solely on Him to either restore strength and heal here on earth or take them on to heaven and give them a perfect new body there (1 Corinthians 15:35–49).

It truly makes no worldly sense to say as Paul did, "I will boast all the more gladly of my weaknesses, so that the power of Christ may rest upon me. For the sake of Christ, then, I am content with weaknesses, insults, hardships, persecutions, and calamities. For when I am weak, then I am strong" (2 Corinthians 12:9–10 ESV), but we have to remember that our faith often won't make any sense in this world; otherwise it wouldn't take *faith*. Consider what 1 Corinthians 1:27–31 (NLT) says: "God chose things the world considers foolish in order to shame those who think they are wise. And he chose things that are powerless to shame those who are powerful. God chose things despised by the world, things counted as nothing at all, and used them to bring to nothing what the world considers important. As a result, no one can ever boast in the presence of God. God has united you with Christ Jesus. For our benefit God made him to be wisdom itself. Christ made us right with God; he made us pure and holy, and he freed us from sin. Therefore, as the Scriptures say, 'If you want to boast, boast only about the LORD.' "

A beautiful woman of God has a weak human body and is weak by herself in every human pursuit—because only then can God make her body truly strong in *His* power and strength.

Giving Up

Give your bodies to God because of all he has done for you.
Let them be a living and holy sacrifice.
ROMANS 12:1 NLT

Many women who are mothers will tell you they gave up their bodies to have children. Obviously childbearing has major effects on the body during the nine months of pregnancy, but it also has the potential for drastic and permanent (and not always welcome) effects, since the female body rarely returns to its exact prepregnancy form. But most mothers will agree that sacrificing their bodies as they once knew them for the sake of having children is absolutely worth it.

Beautiful women of God will agree that giving up their bodies as a sacrifice to God is absolutely worth it, too. In Romans 12:1–2 (NLT), we are called to do so: "And so, dear brothers and sisters, I plead with you to give your bodies to

God because of all he has done for you. Let them be a living and holy sacrifice—the kind he will find acceptable. This is truly the way to worship him. Don't copy the behavior and customs of this world, but let God transform you into a new person by changing the way you think. Then you will learn to know God's will for you, which is good and pleasing and perfect."

Sacrificing our bodies to God is not some scary-sounding religious ritual; it simply means giving up our selfish human nature and the ways of this world in order to follow after Jesus. Some women in today's world take offense at the thought of giving any part of themselves up for another, but God only asks because He loves us dearly, and when we give Him control of our lives, He leads us in His perfect plan for us.

We must realize what Elisabeth Elliot once said: "It is this body that is the primary material given to us for sacrifice. We cannot give our hearts to God and keep our bodies for ourselves."

Well Dressed

"Consider the lilies of the field. . . ."
MATTHEW 6:28 ESV

*E*rma Bombeck hilariously once said, "I never leaf through a copy of *National Geographic* without realizing how lucky we are to live in a society where it is traditional to wear clothes." I think most women would agree with Erma! On the other hand, it can be a challenge to try to keep up with the latest fashion trends, not to mention expensive. But still, clothes are nice.

As women of God, we don't have to try to look like runway models. Some of us enjoy being fashionable and that's fine. Some of us couldn't care less if our wardrobe consists of only T-shirts and jeans—and that's fine, too. What matters is that we don't become obsessed with clothing, neither worrying if we will have enough to wear nor if we will have the latest fashions to wear. Jesus said, "Therefore I tell you, do not be anxious about your life, what you will eat or what you will drink, nor about your body, what you will put on. Is not life more than food, and the body more than clothing? . . . And why are you anxious about clothing? Consider the lilies of the field, how they grow: they neither toil nor spin, yet I tell you, even Solomon in all his glory was not arrayed like one of these. But if God so clothes the grass of the field, which today is alive and tomorrow is thrown into the oven, will he not much more clothe you, O you of little faith? Therefore do not be anxious, saying, 'What shall we eat?' or 'What shall we drink?' or 'What shall we wear?' For the Gentiles seek after all these things, and your heavenly Father knows that you need them all. But seek first the kingdom of God and his righteousness, and all these things will be added to you" (Matthew 6:25–33 ESV).

Beautiful women of God will always be well dressed, because God will never stop providing.

Bowed Down

O come, let us worship and bow down:
let us kneel before the LORD our maker.
PSALM 95:6 KJV

Sometimes the demands and stress of life make us feel like we'd like to lie down on the floor and never get back up. Actually, sometimes facedown on the floor is the best place we can be—if it means we're putting our bodies in a position of humility as we talk to our almighty God.

The Bible tells us to be in constant prayer, so that means we're often just praying to God as we go about our day—sharing bits and pieces of a running conversation with Him, sometimes out loud, sometimes silently in our hearts and minds. And that's great! But we also must remember to take time frequently to focus *completely* on communicating with God and literally bow our bodies before Him. He is the King of kings and the Lord of lords! Thankfully, because of Jesus, we can come before His throne with confidence (Hebrews 4:16), but we should also remember at times to literally humble ourselves before Him (James 4:10) and kneel down like Paul did (Ephesians 3:14) in prayer and praise to our great God. Remember these beautiful words of Psalm 95 as you bow before Him:

For the LORD is the great God, the great King above all gods. In his hand are the depths of the earth, and the mountain peaks belong to him. The sea is his, for he made it, and his hands formed the dry land. Come, let us bow down in worship, let us kneel before the LORD our Maker; for he is our God and we are the people of his pasture, the flock under his care. (Psalm 95:3–7 NIV)

*I think growing older is
a wonderful privilege.
I want to learn to glorify
God in every stage of my life.*

GEORGE MacDONALD

Beautiful Always,
Aging Gracefully

Going Gray

Gray hair is a crown of splendor;
it is attained in the way of righteousness.
PROVERBS 16:31 NIV

Most of us aren't happy to find the first gray hairs on our heads. It's a sign of aging that we just don't want to believe—and a good reason to call our hairdresser or beeline for the hair-care aisle for some DIY hair dye. But the Bible says gray hair is a crown of splendor, or as most other translations put it, a crown of glory, and Proverbs 20:29 (NLT) says, "The glory of the young is their strength; the gray hair of experience is the splendor of the old." So why do we dread gray hair so? Because our world worships youth, and it has for generations. There have even been legends and stories for thousands of years in many cultures about an elusive fountain of youth that makes anyone who drinks its waters young again.

Our culture makes us *desperately* want to hold on to our youth. Maybe the reason for this is that most people in our culture are afraid of aging because aging eventually means death—and death without the Savior (whom most people, sadly, don't know) is extremely scary.

But a beautiful woman of God can delight in her graying hair, even if she does choose to dye it. She can delight in the fact that it's there under the color; she can delight in the fact that she's aging. Why? Because it means she's that much closer to heaven, to eternity in a perfect paradise in the presence of God, where she will never grow old again.

Heavenly Bodies

Our bodies are buried in brokenness,
but they will be raised in glory.
1 CORINTHIANS 15:43 NLT

As we get older, more than just our hair changes in appearance. Like the Bible says, "our bodies are buried in brokenness." But we don't need to go into all the depressing details of that. Rather than lament the loss of a young body, we need to focus on the fact that as our earthly bodies age, they are simply showing signs of stepping closer and closer into eternity. And we should actually take joy in that, not fear it, because if we have accepted salvation through Jesus Christ, then we will spend eternity in heaven with Him in a perfect heavenly body.

We can find great encouragement in 2 Corinthians 5:1–5 (NLT): "For we know that when this earthly tent we live in is taken down (that is, when we die and leave this earthly body), we will have a house in heaven, an eternal body made for us by God himself and not by human hands. We grow weary in our present bodies, and we long to put on our heavenly bodies like new clothing. For we will put on heavenly bodies; we will not be spirits without bodies. While we live in these earthly bodies, we groan and sigh, but it's not that we want to die and get rid of these bodies that clothe us. Rather, we want to put on our new bodies so that these dying bodies will be swallowed up by life. God himself has prepared us for this, and as a guarantee he has given us his Holy Spirit."

These earthly bodies that age and change are only temporary. A woman who is beautiful to God has a perfect, ageless body waiting for her in heaven.

Never Too Old

And let us not grow weary while doing good.
GALATIANS 6:9 NKJV

After being rescued from a Nazi concentration camp, Holocaust survivor and hero of the faith Corrie ten Boom could have retired from working for God. She and her family had helped save the lives of countless Jews and put themselves in grave danger and were eventually imprisoned for doing so. After all the horrors she'd suffered, who would have blamed her for just wanting to quietly relax for the rest of her life? But instead, Corrie began working for the Lord with new enthusiasm, feeling called to share her and her family's story with the world. She traveled the globe speaking and evangelizing, writing books, making movies, and ministering to those around her until the day she died on her ninety-first birthday, even though she had suffered multiple strokes and couldn't actually speak for the last five years of her life. In those final years she encouraged everyone around her by communicating with her eyes and with silent prayer.

We may not all have the calling or stamina or incredible story of Corrie ten Boom, but her example inspires us with the truth that, as we get older, we should never give up working for God. No matter our physical abilities, He can always use us. Galatians 6:9–10 (NIV) says, "Let us not become weary in doing good, for at the proper time we will reap a harvest if we do not give up. Therefore, as we have opportunity, let us do good to all people, especially to those who belong to the family of believers."

A beautiful woman of God may lose every bit of her physical beauty as she ages, but she will never lose her beautiful heart and spirit, her desire to do God's will.

All Generations

Now to him who is able to do far more abundantly than all that we ask or think, according to the power at work within us, to him be glory in the church and in Christ Jesus throughout all generations, forever and ever. Amen.
EPHESIANS 3:20–21 ESV

*E*ach new generation that grows up can make us feel older and older as we observe them with their new technology, new styles and fads, and even what seems like a whole new language at times. It can be overwhelming to try to stay connected with younger generations—but we still need to try. No, we shouldn't try too hard to fit in, pretending to be eighteen again when we're really pushing fifty. We need to be content with whatever age we are and just be ourselves, but we can always seek to understand the younger generations. We need to make ourselves available to them, offering the wisdom we have learned from life experience and guidance to help them on their life's journey. Of course we can't force advice down their throats, but women of God will want to reach out to other women of every age. And we cannot do that if we have no clue how to connect with them and no idea what issues they are really facing. We need to listen and respect them for who they are, even if their latest fads and fashions might repel us. And in turn they just might listen and respect us more, too.

Think how different our culture is today compared to Bible times. It's mind boggling! And yet the Jesus who came in human form back then is the same Jesus on the throne of heaven now and the same Jesus who will come back for us in the future. Luke 1:50 (NIV) says, "His mercy extends to those who fear him, from generation to generation."

His love for people never changes with the changing of the times. And as beautiful women of God, we should make sure our love for people always remains constant, too.

Finding the Funny

No wonder my heart is glad, and I rejoice.
PSALM 16:9 NLT

Laugh a lot, and when you're older all your wrinkles will be in the right places." What a fun quote that is! As we age, we need to make sure we never stop laughing, especially at ourselves. If we take ourselves too seriously, we'll only cause stress for ourselves and those around us. Who wants to be around someone who is always complaining and negative? In the same way, someone who jokes too much can be extremely annoying. We have to find that good balance of knowing when to be serious and sincere and when to relax and focus on the funny in life. Even in a tough situation, we can look for the humor to keep our hearts light, rejoicing in the peace of mind that comes from knowing no matter what comes our way, God never lets us go. He has promised, "I will never leave you nor forsake you" (Hebrews 13:5 ESV).

Psalm 16:5–11 (NLT) is a beautiful passage reminding us of lighthearted joy, reminding us that as women who belong to the Lord, we can delight in aging and never stop laughing, for God is good, and we are His: "LORD, you alone are my inheritance, my cup of blessing. You guard all that is mine. The land you have given me is a pleasant land. What a wonderful inheritance! I will bless the LORD who guides me; even at night my heart instructs me. I know the LORD is always with me. I will not be shaken, for he is right beside me. No wonder my heart is glad, and I rejoice. My body rests in safety. For you will not leave my soul among the dead or allow your holy one to rot in the grave. You will show me the way of life, granting me the joy of your presence and the pleasures of living with you forever."

Beautiful Memories

Remember the former things, those of long ago; I am God, and there is no other; I am God, and there is none like me.
ISAIAH 46:9 NIV

Many of us know the old hymn "Count Your Blessings," written in 1897 by Johnson Oatman Jr. The lyrics to the chorus go like this:

> Count your blessings, name them one by one;
> Count your blessings, see what God hath done!
> Count your blessings, name them one by one;
> And it will surprise you what the Lord hath
>   done.

As we age, we have more and more blessings to count, because God never stops providing for us, giving gifts to us, and guiding us through difficult times. Psalm 63:2–6 (NIV) says, "I have seen you in the sanctuary and beheld your power and your glory. Because your love is better than life, my lips will glorify you. I will praise you as long as I live, and in your name I will lift up my hands. I will be fully satisfied as with the richest of foods; with singing lips my mouth will praise you. On my bed I remember you; I think of you through the watches of the night." What good or gratitude is there in forgetting what God has done for us? No, we should constantly remember His blessings and share them with others, too—especially when it will help encourage someone going through a rough time who could benefit from hearing our own experiences of God working in our lives.

Counting our blessings helps keep our memories sharp and makes us remember that if God has provided in the past, He will certainly provide for whatever we face in the present or the future. As Rick Warren has said, "Remember how far you've come, not just how far you have to go."

And in our final days, when our memories might have faded completely, beautiful women of God need only to say like John Newton did, "My memory is nearly gone; but I remember two things; that I am a great sinner, and that Christ is a great Savior."